THE COLLEGE MUSIC SOCIETY

GEORGE GERSHWIN

A SELECTIVE BIBLIOGRAPHY AND DISCOGRAPHY

BY CHARLES SCHWARTZ

THE COLLEGE MUSIC SOCIETY

BIBLIOGRAPHIES IN AMERICAN MUSIC   NUMBER 1

Detroit   1974   Published for The College Music Society by Information Coordinators

GEORGE GERSHWIN

A SELECTIVE BIBLIOGRAPHY AND DISCOGRAPHY

BY CHARLES SCHWARTZ

THE COLLEGE MUSIC SOCIETY

BIBLIOGRAPHIES IN AMERICAN MUSIC   NUMBER 1

Detroit   1974   Information Coordinators

Portrait of George Gershwin by
Grancel Fitz, New York

Copyright © 1974 by The College Music Society, Inc.
Library of Congress Catalog Card Number 74-75913
International Standard Book Number 911772-59-6

Printed and bound in the United States of America
Designed by Vincent Kibildis
Published for The College Music Society by
Information Coordinators
1435-37 Randolph Street
Detroit, Michigan 48226

CONTENTS

PREFACE

THE COLLEGE MUSIC SOCIETY takes great pride in launching this new series of *Bibliographies in American Music* of which the present publication is the first. In the fifteen years since its founding, the Society has taken seriously its stated constitutional purpose "to gather, consider, and disseminate ideas on the philosophy and practice of music as an integral part of higher education." During this period, its other publications such as the annual journal *College Music Symposium,* and the biennial *Directory of Music Faculties in Colleges and Universities, United States and Canada* have well served these purposes of the Society and those of the profession as a whole. Now, in an era when the interest of American music faculties turns more and more toward the study and transmission of our own cultural heritage, it seems entirely appropriate that the Society should begin to provide primary source material in the form of these bibliographies by means of which further research and instruction can take place. It is all the more appropriate that CMS should join with many other scholarly and professional organizations in celebrating the 200th anniversary of our nation's birth in an appropriate manner.

As the present volume marks the 75th anniversary of the birth of George Gershwin, so will future publications in this series mark important dates in American music such as the Charles Ives centennial in 1974. Other volumes in the series will present bibliographic information on the lives and works of many major American composers, on first performances in the United States of important musical compositions, on the role of music in American higher education, and on other similar subjects. The Society sincerely hopes that this series and its other activities will carry forward its distinguished tradition of service to the cause of music in American higher education and to those dedicated persons who practice it on a daily basis.

Walter S. Collins
President
College Music Society

INTRODUCTION

IT IS PERHAPS only fitting that the first issue of *Bibliographies in American Music* should include a George Gershwin bibliography, inasmuch as the 75th anniversary of the composer's birth, on September 26, 1973, occurs almost concurrently with this issue. In a sense, this issue of the *Bibliographies* can be considered an anniversary issue because of the timely inclusion of a Gershwin bibliography. After all, what better way to honor Gershwin and his achievements than through a compilation of some of the many sources that deal with his life and work? But anniversary issue or not, the CMS deserves the commendation and thanks of its many subscribers and followers for undertaking this important new series.

During his lifetime, George Gershwin was frequently in the news, especially after the extraordinary success of the *Rhapsody in Blue* in 1924. Reports about his eventful private life and his hectic activities as composer, pianist, and conductor were widely and steadily circulated by the press, both as a means of satisfying public interest in him and because he was invariably such good copy. These press reports, of course, only added to his popularity. His career, moreover, epitomized the American Horatio Alger tale of success. For despite humble origins (he was born in Brooklyn, in 1898, to Russian-Jewish parents of modest means), Gershwin rose to international fame. Along the way, he accumulated considerable personal wealth and hobnobbed, too, with many of the leading celebrities of his day. His life contained many of the germinal elements from which legends grow. These elements were dramatically stimulated by his sudden death in 1937, from a brain tumor, at the peak of his physical and creative powers.

The tremendous amount of attention and publicity accorded Gershwin while he lived has continued since his death. As a matter of fact, he and his music are probably better known now than ever before. Some evidence of Gershwin's ever-growing popularity can be seen from the U. S. postage stamp recently issued in his honor; the Hollywood movie of his life (the highly fictional *Rhapsody in Blue,* released in 1945); the number of buildings and schools named after him throughout the country; the broad appeal of numerous television specials which are based on his music; the success of George Balanchine's 1970 ballet, *Who*

Cares?, which features seventeen of his song hits; the music competitions that use his name; and the many all-Gershwin concerts which attract capacity audiences throughout the world—to cite but a few examples.

As the hero of his own bigger-than-life drama, Gershwin has been the subject of numerous biographical studies. It is readily evident from the many biographies and monographs of assorted lengths and quality, plus countless press reports, reviews, articles, and program notes, that the subject of George Gershwin is amply covered in a variety of languages: English, French, German, Russian, and others. In addition to the wide range of published materials, he has been the focus of considerable attention in the repositories of memorabilia, scores and other Gershwiniana such as those found in the Music and Theater Divisions of The New York Public Library, the Gershwin Collection in the Music Division of The Library of Congress, the George and Ira Gershwin Collection at the Museum of the City of New York, and the George Gershwin Memorial Collection at Fisk University. The Gershwin bibliographic cup truly runneth over!

With so much written material about Gershwin, it is surprising that many aspects of his life and work are not as clear as they might be. Unquestionably these cloudy areas stem in large part from the normal problems of evaluation and interpretation of biographical and musical material. But these problems have been intensified in Gershwin's case by the extraordinary amount of publicity he received over the years. Thus, as a cumulative result of reiterated anecdotes and viewpoints about Gershwin, an image of him as man and musician has been established as a "definitive" one, even though it does not provide a true picture of him. Another source of difficulty in placing Gershwin in proper perspective has to do with the large quantity of derivative literature which draws heavily upon personal studies which are essentially partial in outlook, such as Isaac Goldberg's biography, *GEORGE GERSHWIN: A Study in American Music.* This "authorized" biography was written with Gershwin's approval and full cooperation. It was published in 1931 when the composer was only thirty-three and was the first major study of his life and work. Like Goldberg, such key Gershwin biographers as Oscar Levant, David Ewen, and Merle Armitage were close personal friends; similarly, Edward Jablonski and Lawrence D. Stewart—authors of *The Gershwin Years* and members of a younger generation—are good friends of Ira Gershwin. All their biographies reflect, in one way or another, these personal relationships, although their works, to be sure, have considerable substance. Nevertheless, their treatment of Gershwin's life is not always as accurate or as objective as one might wish. Their analyses and evaluation of Gershwin's music has, in turn, displayed deficiencies in musical scholarship.

Despite these reservations, the overall Gershwin bibliography has much to commend it. For it is rich with on-the-spot press reports and reviews, and first-hand accounts of the composer by his friends and colleagues. Because of the amplitude of the material on Gershwin, a "complete" Gershwin bibliography is probably not realizable. For practical purposes, a "selected" bibliography, derived largely from sources culled by this writer for his doctoral dissertation on the composer's life and music, which served as the basis for a book on Gershwin (*GERSHWIN: His Life and Music*) published in 1973 by Bobbs-Merrill, has been compiled here. Since this compilation has been taken from a massive literature, there are bound to be occasional gaps. For example, only a few doctoral dissertations which deal in part, directly or indirectly, with Gershwin have been given, and only a relative sampling of contemporary reviews of Gershwin's major works have been cited. Similarly, only a few dictionary articles have been listed. RILM citations, however, have been given wherever known, as they provide comprehensive abstracts; and descriptive annotations have been added to a number of bibliographic citations.

Organization of the bibliography proper is entirely alphabetical by author (or title, when author is unknown). In cases where authors have written more than one item (*e.g.,* Edward Jablonski, Isaac Goldberg, Edward N. Waters), their collective contribution is organized in chronological order; in this way one can easily see Irving Kolodin's continued interest in Gershwin matters from 1935 to 1971. Finally, entries of special interest have been marked with an asterisk (*).

This writer would like to warmly thank Frederick Freedman, of Case Western Reserve University, for his invaluable editorial assistance. His incisive critical comments were consistently of great value. Thanks, too, are in order for two of his former assistants, Stephanie Tretick and Cynthia Dyballa, whose cooperation went beyond the call of duty. This writer would like to note also that he is delighted to be able to contribute to *Bibliographies in American Music.* Long may this very valuable series continue.

Charles Schwartz

New York
September 1973

1898—George Gershwin was born on September 26 at 242 Snediker Avenue, between Sutter and Belmont Avenues, in the East New York section of Brooklyn shortly after his parents and older brother Ira had moved there from Manhattan.

c.1900—The Gershwins moved back to Manhattan. The composer grew up on the lower East Side.

c.1910—Gershwin began the study of piano with neighborhood piano teachers.

1913—Gershwin showed his interest in popular music by writing "Since I Found You" and "Ragging the Traumerei," both with lyrics by Leonard Praskins. Neither song has been published.

1914—In May, Gershwin left high school for employment at Remick's, a publisher of popular music, as a song "plugger."

1916—Gershwin signed a contract on March 1 with the Harry von Tilzer Publishing Company for the publication of "When You Want 'Em, You Can't Get 'Em, When You Got 'Em, You Don't Want 'Em," lyrics by Murray Roth. This was Gershwin's first published song.

1917—Gershwin left Remick's on March 17 to make his career as a tunesmith.

1918—In February, Max Dreyfus, head of T. B. Harms, one of the most important publishers in Tin Pan Alley, offered Gershwin an exclusive contract to write songs for his company. With Harms as his publisher, Gershwin made rapid strides in the popular music field.

1919—The first musical for which Gershwin wrote the complete score was *La, La, Lucille* (book by Fred Jackson; lyrics by Arthur Jackson and B. G. De Sylva). Produced by Alex A. Aarons, *La, La, Lucille* opened at the Henry Miller Theater on May 26 and ran for 104 performances.

1920—"Swanee" (lyrics, Irving Caesar) became Gershwin's first big song hit after Al Jolson incorporated the tune into his musical *Sinbad* and also recorded it on January 8, 1920 for Columbia Records. Originally "Swanee" met with little success when it was included in the *Capitol Revue,* a revue presented in connection with the opening of the Capitol Theater, a movie house, on October 24, 1919.

1920—Gershwin wrote the score for the first of five annual George White's *Scandals* (from 1920 until 1924). *George White's Scandals of 1920* (book by Andy Rice and George White; lyrics by Arthur Jackson) opened at the Globe Theater on June 7, 1920 and ran for 318 performances.

1922—Gershwin tried his hand at writing a one-act opera, *Blue Monday Blues,* to a libretto by B. G. De Sylva, for *George White's Scandals of 1922.* The opera was withdrawn from the *Scandals* after its Broadway opening on August 28, 1922. (Retitled *135th Street* and orchestrated by Ferde Grofé, the opera received its concert hall premiere on December 29, 1925, at Carnegie Hall, by Paul Whiteman's Orchestra.)

1923—Gershwin appeared in concert with Eva Gauthier, soprano, at Aeolian Hall on November 1 in a program of art and popular songs. Gershwin was singled out for praise both as pianist and tunesmith. This concert helped demonstrate that popular music could be accepted in the concert hall.

1924—The highly successful premiere of the *Rhapsody in Blue* "for jazz band and piano" on February 12 at Aeolian Hall helped to make Gershwin world famous. The work, orchestrated by Ferde Grofé, was performed by Paul Whiteman and his Palais Royal Orchestra, with Gershwin as pianist, in a concert billed as "an experiment in modern music."

1924—Gershwin wrote the music for *Lady, Be Good* to his brother Ira's lyrics, the first complete score they wrote together. Among the famous tunes from this score are "Fascinating Rhythm" and "Oh, Lady Be Good!" From this show onward, Ira wrote the lyrics for nearly all George's tunes. *Lady, Be Good* (book by Guy Bolton and Fred Thompson) ran for 184 performances after it opened at the Liberty Theater on December 1 and helped to catapult Fred and Adele Astaire to stardom. Alex A. Aarons and Vinton Freedley produced *Lady, Be Good* as well as *Tip-Toes* (1925), *Oh, Kay!* (1926), *Funny Face* (1927), *Treasure Girl* (1928), *Girl Crazy* (1930), and *Pardon My English* (1933)—all with Gershwin scores. Aarons and Freedley were Gershwin's most important producers until the dissolution of their partnership in 1933.

1925—The premiere of the *Concerto in F* for piano and orchestra on December 3 at Carnegie Hall. Walter Damrosch conducted the New York Symphony Orchestra, with Gershwin as pianist.

1925—*Tip-Toes*, for which George and Ira Gershwin wrote the score, opened at the Liberty Theater on December 28 and ran for 194 performances. "Sweet and Low-Down," "Looking for a Boy," and "That Certain Feeling" are some of the tunes from this score.

1926—*Oh, Kay!*, with a Gershwin score that included "Clap Yo' Hands," "Maybe," "Someone to Watch over Me," and "Do, Do, Do," opened at the Imperial Theater on November 8. Starring Gertrude Lawrence, this musical ran for 256 performances.

1926—Gershwin performed five preludes for piano for the first time on December 4 at New York's Hotel Roosevelt in a recital he gave with Marguerite d'Alvarez, contralto. Three of these preludes became the famous *Preludes for Piano* and were published in 1927.

1927—Fred and Adele Astaire starred in Aarons and Freedley's *Funny Face*. In addition to the title tune, the Gershwin score for the show included " 'S Wonderful" and "The Babbitt and the Bromide." *Funny Face* opened at the Alvin Theater on November 22 and ran for 244 performances.

1928—"I've Got a Crush on You" and "Feeling I'm Falling" were included in the Gershwin score for *Treasure Girl*, which starred Gertrude Lawrence. *Treasure Girl* opened at the Alvin Theater on November 8 and ran for 68 performances.

1928—The premiere of *An American in Paris*, a tone poem for orchestra, took place on December 13 at Carnegie Hall by the New York Philharmonic conducted by Walter Damrosch.

1929—"Liza" was among the tunes Gershwin wrote for the score of *Show Girl* (lyrics by Ira Gershwin and Gus Kahn), a Ziegfeld production which featured Ruby Keeler and Clayton, Jackson, and Durante. *Show Girl* opened at the Ziegfeld Theater on July 2, 1929 and ran for 111 performances.

1930—*Strike Up the Band* (second version; the first version closed out of town in 1927 and never reached Broadway), with a Gershwin score and a book by Morrie Ryskind (adapted from a book by George S. Kaufman) opened at the Times Square Theater on January 14 and ran for 191 performances. The title song, "I've Got a Crush on You," and "Soon" are some of the memorable tunes from this musical.

1930—The Aarons-Freedley production of *Girl Crazy*, with a Gershwin score and a cast that included Ethel Merman and Ginger Rogers, opened at the Alvin Theater on October 14 and ran for 272 performances. "Bidin' My Time," "But Not for Me," "Embraceable You," and "I Got Rhythm" are among the Gershwin tunes in the score.

1931—The Hollywood film *Delicious*, starring Janet Gaynor and Charles Farrell and with a Gershwin score that included an orchestral excerpt that was the basis for the *Second Rhapsody*, was released on December 3.

1931—*Of Thee I Sing*, the musical satire on American politics, opened at the Music Box Theater on December 26. Based on a book by George S. Kaufman and Morrie Ryskind and with a Gershwin score, *Of Thee I Sing* starred William Gaxton, Victor Moore, and Lois Moran. It ran for 441 performances, longer than any other Gershwin musical. On May 2, 1932, *Of Thee I Sing* received a Pulitzer Prize in drama, the first musical comedy to be so honored. Among the famous Gershwin tunes in the score are "Love Is Sweeping the Country," the title song, "Who Cares?," and "Wintergreen for President."

1932—The *Second Rhapsody* "for orchestra with piano" was premiered at Boston's Symphony Hall on January 29 by the Boston Symphony Orchestra under Serge Koussevitzky, with Gershwin as pianist. (The *Second Rhapsody* was completed on May 23, 1931.)

1932—The premiere of the *Cuban Overture* (originally titled *Rumba*) for orchestra was performed on August 16 at Lewisohn Stadium (NY), with Albert Coates conducting the New York Philharmonic.

1932—Simon and Schuster published (September 1932) *George Gershwin's Song-Book*, piano transcriptions of "improvisations" of eighteen famous songs by the composer, ranging from "Swanee" to "Who Cares?"

1933—*Let 'Em Eat Cake*, the sequel to *Of Thee I Sing*, opened at the Imperial Theater on October 21. Unlike *Of Thee I Sing*, *Let 'Em Eat Cake* closed after only 90 performances. Included in the Gershwin score was the famous tune "Mine."

1934—The premiere of the *"I Got Rhythm" Variations* for piano and orchestra on January 14 was performed at Boston's Symphony Hall by the Leo Reisman Orchestra conducted by Charles Previn, with Gershwin as soloist.

1935—Gershwin's opera *Porgy and Bess*, based on DuBose Heyward's novel *Porgy*, opened at the Alvin Theater on October 10. Produced by the Theatre Guild, with Todd Duncan as Porgy and Anne Wiggins Brown as Bess, the opera ran for 124 performances on Broadway, with Alexander Smallens conducting.

1936—The premiere of *Catfish Row*, a five-movement suite for orchestra adapted by Gershwin from *Porgy and Bess*, took place on January 21 at Philadelphia's Academy of Music, with Alexander Smallens conducting the Philadelphia Orchestra.

1937—*Shall We Dance*, an RKO film starring Fred Astaire and Ginger Rogers was released on May 7. The Gershwin score for this film contains "(I've Got) Beginner's Luck," "Let's Call the Whole Thing Off," "Shall We Dance," "Slap that Bass," "They All Laughed," "They Can't Take That Away from Me," all with lyrics by Ira Gershwin, plus an instrumental interlude "Walking the Dog" (the latter was first published in 1960 as a piano solo, titled "Promenade").

1937—Gershwin completed the score for *A Damsel in Distress*, another Astaire film by RKO, before his death in July. *A Damsel in Distress* was released on November 19, 1937 and included these Gershwin tunes: "A Foggy Day," "Nice Work If You Can Get It," "Stiff Upper Lip," and "Things Are Looking Up."

1937—Gershwin did not quite complete the score for the movie *The Goldwyn Follies* before his death; Vernon Duke was called in by Samuel Goldwyn, the producer of the film, to finish the job. When *The Goldwyn Follies*, which featured Adolphe Menjou and Vera Zorina, was released on February 23, 1938, these Gershwin tunes (with lyrics by Ira Gershwin) were heard: "I Love to Rhyme," "I Was Doing All Right," "Love Is Here to Stay," and "Love Walked In."

1937—Gershwin died on July 11 at the Cedars of Lebanon Hospital in Los Angeles after an operation for a brain tumor. His body was brought to New York for funeral services at Manhattan's Temple Emanu-El on July 15. While approximately 3,500 people—most of them prominent in the music world, the theater, and politics—filled huge Emanu-El for the New York services, many of filmdom's big names crowded Hollywood's B'nai B'rith Temple for equally impressive services on the West Coast. After the services, held concurrently, Gershwin was buried at the Mount Hope Cemetary, Hastings-on-Hudson, New York. Ira Gershwin, who lives in Beverly Hills, California, has remained active during the past decades looking after George's interests, as well as continuing his own role as lyricist.

BIBLIOGRAPHY

A

"American Classic Sings Anew," *Life* XLVI/24 (June 15, 1959), 70-77.   1
 Discusses the motion picture *Porgy and Bess.*

AMIS, John. "Opera: Mozart to Gershwin: 'Porgy and Bess'," *The*   2
 Musical Times XCIII [=No. 1317] (Nov 1952), 512-13.

ANTHEIL, George. "The Foremost American Composer," in: Merle   3
 ARMITAGE, ed, *George Gershwin* (NY: Longmans, Green, 1938),
 115-19.

ANTRIM, Doran K. "Fortunes in Melody," *Etude* LX/1 (Jan 1942), 11-12. 4
 Mentions Gershwin's good fortune in *Rhapsody in Blue.*

ARDOIN, John. "Warfield Outstanding in 'Porgy and Bess'," *Musical*   5
 America LXXXI/7 (July 1961), 45.

ARLEN, Harold. "The Composer's Friend," in: Merle ARMITAGE, ed,   6
 George Gershwin (NY: Longmans, Green, 1938), 121-22.

*ARMITAGE, Merle, ed. *George Gershwin.* NY: Longmans, Green, 1938.   7
 252 pp.
 A collection of thirty-eight articles by friends and colleagues of
 Gershwin. Though there are inaccuracies in it, this collection is an
 important source of information about Gershwin.

ARMITAGE, Merle. "George Gershwin and His Time," in: Merle   8
 ARMITAGE, ed, *George Gershwin* (NY: Longmans, Green, 1938),
 5-15.

ARMITAGE, Merle. "George Gershwin," in his: *Accent on America*   **9**
  (NY: E. Weyhe, 1944), 289-98.
  Also a chapter on "Porgy and Bess," 163-66; other citations, 312, 364.

ARMITAGE, Merle. *George Gershwin: Man and Legend,* with a note on   **10**
  the author by John Charles Thomas. NY: Duell, Sloan & Pearce,
  1958. 188 pp. Reprint, Freeport, NY: Books for Libraries Press, 1970.
  Also includes "My Brother" by Ira Gershwin (pp. 11-18), virtually
  unaltered from the Armitage book of 1938. Lists productions of
  Porgy and Bess thru 1958, a brief bibliography, a list of Gershwin's
  works and a discography.

*ARVEY, Verna. "George Gershwin Through the Eyes of a Friend," *Opera* **11**
  and Concert XIII/4 (Apr 1948), 10-11, 27-28.
  The author discusses Kay Swift's friendship with Gershwin.

ARVEY, Verna. "Afro-American Music Memo," *Music Journal* XXVII/9   **12**
  (Nov 1969), 36, 68-69.

The ASCAP Biographical Dictionary. See: "George Gershwin," No. **192.**

*ASTAIRE, Fred. *Steps in Time.* NY: Harper, 1959. 338 pp.   **13**
  Includes some reminiscences by Astaire about his association with
  Gershwin.

"Athens Applauds American Singers in 'Porgy and Bess'," *Musical*   **14**
  America LXXV/3 (Feb 1, 1955), 33.

ATKINSON, Brooks. " 'Porgy and Bess', Native Opera, Opens at the Alvin; **15**
  Gershwin Work Based on Du Bose Heyward's Play: Dramatic Value
  of Community Legend Gloriously Transposed in New Form with
  Fine Regard for Its Verities," *The New York Times* LXXXV/28,384
  (Oct 11, 1935), 30.
  Review of premiere of *Porgy and Bess.*

ATKINSON, Brooks. " 'Of Thee I Sing': Another Production from the   **16**
  Past Is Better than Most of the New Ones," *The New York Times*
  CI/34,441 (May 11, 1952), Sec II, 1.

ATKINSON, Brooks. "Negro Folk Drama: 'Porgy and Bess' Suitable for   **17**
  Production Before Audiences in European Capitals," *The New York
  Times* CL/34,560 (Sep 7, 1952), Sec II, 1.

ATKINSON, Brooks. "Return of a Classic: 'Porgy and Bess' Comes Home **18**
from Europe," *The New York Times* CII/34,749 (Mar 15, 1953),
Sec II, 1.

"Auld Lang Syne," *Musical America* LXXV/3 (Jan 1, 1955), 9. **19**
Porgy and Bess in Belgrade and Zagreb.

AUSTIN, William W. *Music in the Twentieth Century* (NY: W. W. Norton, **20**
1966), 48, 62, 89, 191-92, 384-85, 441, 471, 502-4, 518.

"Austria," *Opera* III/12 (Dec 1952), 733. **21**
Review of *Porgy and Bess.*

B

BAGAR, Robert C. "Rhapsody in Blue," *The Philharmonic-Symphony* **22**
Society of New York [Program] CI/3917 (Dec 24, 25, 27, 1942),
[6-7]. Excerpt in: Robert C. BAGAR (No. **27**), 273-76, under *An
American in Paris.*

BAGAR, Robert C. "Porgy and Bess: A Symphonic Picture [arranged by **23**
Robert Russell Bennett]," *The Philharmonic-Symphony Society
of New York [Program]* CI/3973-74 (Mar 31, Apr 2, 1943), [4-6].
Also in: *Ibid.,* CIII/4309 (Jan 6, 1946), [5-8]. Excerpt in: Robert C.
BAGAR (No. **27**), 273-76, 277-78, under *An American in Paris* &
Porgy and Bess.
Program notes for first NY performance.

BAGAR, Robert C. "An American in Paris," *The Philharmonic-Symphony* **24**
Society of New York [Program] CII/4026-27 (Nov 17, 19, 21, 1943),
[5-7]. Excerpt in: Robert C. BAGAR (No. **27**), 273-76.

BAGAR, Robert C. "I Got Rhythm [Morton Gould orchestral version]," **25**
The Philharmonic-Symphony Society of New York [Program]
CIII/4138 (Oct 8, 1944), [6-8].
Program notes for world premiere of concert performance (previously
heard on radio only).

BAGAR, Robert C. "Concerto for Piano and Orchestra in F Major,"   **26**
   The Philharmonic-Symphony Society of New York [Program]
   CIII/4309 (Jan 6, 1946), [4-5]. Also in: *Ibid.*, CVI (Jan 27, 1949),
   [4-6]. Excerpt in: Robert C. BAGAR (No. **27**), 276-77.

BAGAR, Robert C., & Louis BIANCOLLI. *The Concert Companion*   **27**
   (NY/London: McGraw-Hill, 1947), 273-78.
   > Program notes for *An American in Paris, Concerto in F,* selections
   > from *Porgy and Bess,* & *Rhapsody in Blue;* originally written for
   > the Philharmonic-Symphony Society of New York.

BARAL, Robert. "Irving Berlin's Oldtime Song Hits Most in Demand by   **28**
   Collectors," *Variety* CLXXXI/4 (Jan 3, 1951), 219.

"Barnet's 'Rhapsody' Arrangement Ordered Destroyed by Harms,"   **29**
   Variety CLXXIII/13 (Mar 9, 1949), 48.

BASKERVILLE, David. *Jazz Influence on Art Music to Mid-Century.*   **30**
   Ph.D. Dissertation: University of California at Los Angeles, 1965.
   535 pp. UM: 65-15,175. *Dissertation Abstracts* XXVI/8 (Feb 1966),
   4710-A.
   > Contains a chapter on *Porgy and Bess.*

BAUER, Marion. "The Gershwin Touch," in: *Rhapsody in Blue; the*   **31**
   Jubilant Story of George Gershwin and His Music [Hollywood:
   Warner Bros, 1945], 17.

BECKER, Wolfgang. "Da Berlino," *Nuova Revista Musicale Italiana*   **32**
   IV/2 (Mar-Apr 1970), 343-44.
   > Contains a review of the Berlin performance of *Porgy and Bess.*

*BEHRMAN, Samuel Nathaniel. "Troubadour," *The New Yorker* V/14   **33**
   (May 25, 1929), 27-29. Also as: "Profile," in: Merle ARMITAGE, ed,
   George Gershwin (NY: Longmans, Green, 1938), 211-18.

*BEHRMAN, Samuel Nathaniel. *People in a Diary; a Memoir* (Boston: **34**
   Little, Brown, 1972), 239-58.
   > Gershwin's terminal illness is discussed with great insight.

"Belittling Gershwin," *News-Week* XXVI/8 (Aug 20, 1945), 79.   **35**
   > Critical comments on Gershwin.

BELLERBY, L. "Second Thoughts on Porgy and Bess," *Jazz Journal*   **36**
VI/1 (Jan 1953), 6.

BELLOWS, George Kent. See: John Tasker HOWARD, No. **286**.

"Berlin," *Oper und Konzert* IX/6 (June 1971), 5.   **37**
Review of *Porgy and Bess.*

BERLIN, Irving. "Poem," in: Merle ARMITAGE, ed, *George Gershwin*   **38**
(NY: Longmans, Green, 1938), 78-80.

*BERNSTEIN, Leonard. "A Nice Gershwin Tune," *The Atlantic Monthly*   **39**
CXCV/4 (Apr 1955), 39-42.
Bernstein, in an imaginary conversation with a music-publishing
executive, discusses Gershwin's *An American in Paris, Concerto in F,
Porgy and Bess, & Rhapsody in Blue.*

BERNSTEIN, Leonard. *The Joy of Music.* NY: Simon & Schuster, 1959.   **40**
Bernstein's "A Nice Gershwin Tune" (See: No. **39**) is reprinted here.

BERNSTEIN, Leonard. "Proc si nesednete a nenapisete takovou pisnicku   **41**
jako Gershwin?" *Hudebni Rozhledy* XVIII/16 (1965), 675-77.
Translated from Bernstein's *Joy of Music* (See: No. **40**).

BIANCOLLI, Louis. See: Robert C. BAGAR, No. **27**.

BITTNER, Robert E. *Problems in the Blues, 1920-1930.* Ph.D.   **42**
Dissertation: University of Wisconsin (in progress).

BLESH, Rudi, & Harriet JANIS. *They All Played Ragtime: The True*   **43**
Story of an American Music (NY: A. A. Knopf, 1950), 72, 204.

BLOM, Eric. "George Gershwin," in: *Grove's Dictionary of Music and*   **44**
Musicians, 5th ed, by Eric Blom, 10 vols (London: Macmillan,
1954-61), III, 607; X, 183.

BLUME, Friedrich, ed. *Die Musik in Geschichte und Gegenwart.* See:
Anton WÜRZ, No. **649**.

BLUTHNER, Hans. "'Porgy and Bess' in Berlin," *Jazz Journal* V/11 (Nov   **45**
1952), 12-13.
Reviews performance of the opera at the 1952 Berlin Festival.

*BOLTON, Guy R., & Pelham Grenville WODEHOUSE. *Bring on the*   **46**
    Girls! NY: Simon & Schuster, 1953.
> Two authors of scripts for Gershwin musicals reminisce about the
> composer and their part in Gershwin productions.

BONNER, Eugene. "George Gershwin's Latest," *The Outlook and*   **47**
    Independent CLI/1 (Jan 2, 1929), 34.
> About *An American in Paris.*

BONTEMPS, Arna. See: FISK UNIVERSITY, No. **178.**

BOOKSPAN, Martin. "The Basic Repertoire: Gershwin's *An American in*   **48**
    Paris," *HiFi/Stereo Review* XIV/5 (May 1965), 39-40.
> Comparison of several recordings.

BOOKSPAN, Martin. "The Basic Repertoire: Gershwin's *Rhapsody in*   **49**
    Blue," *HiFi/Stereo Review* XX/2 (Feb 1968), 55-56.
> Comparison of several recordings.

BORISOVA, S. "Molodezh' derzhit ekzamen," *Sovetskaya Muzyka*   **50**
    XXV/5 (May 1961), 53-57.
> About *Porgy and Bess.*

BORNEMAN, Ernest. "Second Thoughts on Some Musical Sacrilege,"   **51**
    Melody Maker XXVIII/998 (Nov 1, 1952), 8.
> Criticising *Porgy and Bess.*

BOROWSKI, Felix. "Concerto in F, for Piano and Orchestra," *Chicago* **52**
    Symphony Orchestra [Program] (Dec 6, 1951), [67-68].

BOSE, Fritz. " 'Porgy and Bess': die Negeroper erstmals auf Platten," **53**
    Musica Schallplatte III/3 (May 1960), 58-59.
> Record review.

*BOTKIN, Henry. "Painter and Collector," in: Merle ARMITAGE, ed,   **54**
    George Gershwin (NY: Longmans, Green, 1938), 137-43.
> Botkin discusses Gershwin's talents as a painter and art collector.

BOURGEOIS, Jacques. "Un disque d'extraits de Porgy and Bess," *Disques* **55**
    VI [= No. 55] (Feb-Mar 1953), 127.
> Record review of *Porgy and Bess.*

BRACKER, Milton. "'Of Thee I Sing' in Modern Dress," *The New York*   **56**
    Times CI/34,434 (May 4, 1952), Sec II, 1, 3.

BRAGGIOTTI, Mario. "Gershwin Is Here to Stay," *Etude* LXXII/2   **57**
    (Feb 1953), 14, 63.
    Includes discussion of his works.

"Bregenzer Festspiele," *Oper und Konzert* IX/9 (Sep 1971), 12.   **58**
    Review of *Porgy and Bess.*

BRIGGS, John. "George Gershwin: A Reappraisal," *Tomorrow* VII/11   **59**
    (July 1948), 20-24.

BROCK. Hella. "Gershwins Oper *Porgy and Bess* in der Musikerziehung;   **60**
    zur Eignung des Werkes für die Schulmusikerziehung," *Musik in
    der Schule* XVIII/12 (Dec 1967), 493-502. RILM[67] 2347.

BUCHANAN, Charles L. "Gershwin and Musical Snobbery," *The Outlook*   **61**
    CXLV/5 (Feb 2, 1927), 146-48.

BUONASSISI, Vincenzo. "Forse nella storia Gershwin," *La Scala* No. 114 **62**
    (May 1959), 43-47, 77-78.
    Summary in French, English & German.

BURK, John N. " 'Porgy and Bess', A Symphonic Picture, Arranged for   **63**
    Orchestra by Robert Russell Bennett," *Concert Bulletin of the
    Boston Symphony Orchestra* LXIII/7 (Nov 26, 27, 1943), 436-44.
    Program notes for the first performance of this work by the BSO.

BURKE, Georgia. "The Porgy and Bess Story, 1952-53," *Equity*   **64**
    XXXVIII/5 (May 1953), 13-15.

BURTON, Jack. "Honor Roll of Popular Songwriters. No. 43—George   **65**
    Gershwin," *Billboard* LXI/47 (Nov 19, 1949), 39; LXI/48 (Nov 26,
    1949), 36; LXI/49 (Dec 3, 1949), 38; LXI/50 (Dec 10, 1949), 40.
    Includes a list of works and discography.

BURTON, Jack. "George Gershwin, 1898-1937," in his: *The Blue Book*   **66**
    of Tin Pan Alley: A Human Interest Anthology of American Popular
    Music (Watkins Glen, NY: Century House, 1950), 292-305.

    Cites all works written by Gershwin, in chronological order, as follows:
    Popular Songs, Stage Musicals, London Musicals, Instrumental
    Numbers, Film Songs, & Scores. Recordings (mainly 78 rpm) of many
    items given.

BURTON, Jack. *The Blue Book of Broadway Musicals.* Watkins Glen,   **67**
    NY: Century House, 1952.

    Details of Gershwin's scores are cited as follows: 110, 179-82,
    249-50, 306.

BURTON, Jack. *The Blue Book of Hollywood Musicals. Songs from the*   **68**
    Sound Tracks and the Stars Who Sang Them Since the Birth of the
    Talkies a Quarter-Century Ago. Watkins Glen, NY: Century House,
    1953.

    Discusses these movies: *Delicious* (1931), 40; *A Damsel in Distress*
    (1937), 94; *Shall We Dance?* (1937), 97; *The Goldwyn Follies*
    (1938), 109; *The Shocking Miss Pilgrim* (1947), 232; *An American*
    in Paris (1951), 263.

BUTTERWORTH, Neil. "American Composers," *Music: The Official*   **69**
    Journal of the Schools Music Association I/4 (1967), 25-26.

    Biography of Gershwin.

BUTTERWORTH, Neil. "American Composers," *Music: The Official*   **70**
    Journal of the Schools Music Association II/1 (1967), 38-40.

" 'Buying American' in Music," *The Literary Digest* CXVIII/26 (Dec 29,   **71**
    1934), 24.

C

CADMAN, B. Meredith. "Gershwin 'Algerized'," *Etude* LXIV/9 (Sep   **72**
    1946), 491.

    Book review of Ewen's *The Story of George Gershwin* (See: No. **157**).

CALTA, Louis. "Stage Folk to See Preview of 'Porgy'," *The New York*   **73**
    Times CII/34,738 (Mar 4, 1953), 21.

*CAMPBELL, Frank C. "The Musical Scores of George Gershwin," *The*   **74**
    Library of Congress Quarterly Journal of Current Acquisitions XI/3
    (May 1954), 127-39.
    Discusses Gershwin's orchestral manuscripts at The Library of
    Congress; includes twenty-two musical examples.

*CAMPBELL, Frank C. "Some Manuscripts of George Gershwin,"   **75**
    Manuscripts (Winter 1954), 66-75.
    Another report of Gershwin's orchestral manuscripts at The Library
    of Congress.

CAMPBELL-WATSON, Frank. "Preamble" to *"I Got Rhythm"*   **76**
    Variations, rev by William C. Schoenfeld (NY: New World Music
    Corp, 1953).

CAPOTE, Truman. "Onward and Upward With the Arts: I—When the   **77**
    Cannons Are Silent: Porgy and Bess in Russia," *The New Yorker*
    XXXII/35 (Oct 20, 1956), 38-40, 42, 44, 47-49, 52, 54, 56, 58,
    60-62, 65-66, 69-70, 72, 74, 76, 78-80, 83-100, 105.
    First part of two-part article.

*CAPOTE, Truman. *The Muses Are Heard, an Account.* NY: Random   **78**
    House, 1956. 182 pp.
    Capote's account of performances of *Porgy and Bess* in Russia.

CARUTHERS, Osgood. "Catfish Row à la Soviet," *The New York Times* **79**
    CX/37,745 (May 28, 1961), Sec II, 3.
    About an unauthorized Russian version of *Porgy and Bess.*

"Casting Woes for Prawy's 'Porgy'; Sells Out Every Repeat Performance," **80**
    Variety CCLVI/11 (Oct 29, 1969), 75.

"Catfish Row in an Encore," *News-Week* XIX/5 (Feb 2, 1942), 55-57.   **81**
    Review of the revival of *Porgy and Bess* at New York's Majestic Theatre.

CAVENDISH, Thomas H. *Folk Music in Selected Twentieth Century*   **82**
    American Opera. Ph.D. Dissertation: Florida State University, 1966.
    209 pp. UM: 67-343. *Dissertation Abstracts* XXVIII/3 (Sep 1967),
    1093-A.

*CERF, Bennett. "In Memory of George Gershwin," *Saturday Review of* **83**
    Literature XXVI/29 (July 17, 1943), 14-16.
    In his usual witty style, Cerf tells some anecdotes about Gershwin.

CERF, Bennett. *Try and Stop Me.* NY: Simon & Schuster, 1944. 378 pp.   **84**
   Cerf's "In Memory of George Gershwin" is incorporated into this
   book of anecdotes.

CHALUPT, René. *George Gershwin, le musicien de la "Rhapsody in*   **85**
   Blue." Paris: Amiot-Dumont, 1948. 175 pp. Italian translation by
   Robert Leydi as: *Gershwin.* Milan: Nuova Accademia, 1959. 211 pp.

"Charleston (and Gershwin) Provide Folk-Opera." *The Literary Digest*   **86**
   CXX/17 (Oct 26, 1935), 18.

CHASE, Gilbert. *America's Music from the Pilgrims to the Present,* 2nd ed **87**
   (NY: McGraw-Hill, 1966), 462, 488-95, 517, 518, 622, 630, 642-45.
   1st ed, 1955.
   Includes discussion of *Porgy and Bess* & *Rhapsody in Blue.*

CHASE, Gilbert, ed. *The American Composer Speaks: A Historical*   **88**
   Anthology, 1770-1965 (Baton Rouge, La: Louisiana State University
   Press, 1966), 3, 5, 13, 26, 139-40, 260.
   Includes an introduction to Gershwin's article "The Composer in the
   Machine Age." RILM[67] 76.

CHASINS, Abram. "Paradox in Blue," *Saturday Review of Literature*   **89**
   XXXIX/8 (Feb 25, 1956), 37, 39, 64-66.

CLAUSEN, Bernard C. "Strike Up the Band," *Christian Century* XLVIII/   **90**
   26 (July 8, 1931), 899-901.

COE, Richard L. " 'Porgy' at La Scala Just Another Wow Date; SRO Show   **91**
   Eyes Tent Setup," *Variety* CXCVIII/1 (Mar 9, 1955), 2+.

COEUROY, André. *Panorama de la musique Contemporaine* (Paris: Les   **92**
   Documentaires, 1928), 65, 70.
   Remarks on Gershwin & jazz.

"Composer's Pictures," *Arts and Decorations* XL (Jan 1934), 48-50.   **93**

"Congressman Attacks 'Porgy' Tour, Despite Show's Favorable Impact,"   **94**
   Variety CCI/2 (Dec 14, 1955), 1+.

COPLAND, Aaron. *What to Listen for in Music.* NY/London: Whittlesey   **95**
House, McGraw-Hill, 1939, 1953.

COPLAND, Aaron. *Our New Music* (NY/London: Whittlesey House,   **96**
McGraw-Hill, 1941), 85, 99. Rev ed as: *The New Music, 1900-1960*
(NY: W. W. Norton, 1968), 61, 70.

  Brief passing remarks.

COWELL, Henry. *American Composers on American Music.* Palo Alto: **97**
Stanford University Press, 1933. Reprint with a new introduction,
NY: Frederick Ungar, 1962. See: George GERSHWIN, No. **212**.

CRAFT, Robert. See: Igor STRAVINSKY, Nos. **560** & **561**.

CROCE, Arlene. *The Fred Astaire and Ginger Rogers Book.* NY: **98**
Outerbridge & Lazard (distributed by Dutton), 1972. 191 pp.

  Gives information about the films *Shall We Dance?* and *A Damsel
in Distress,* both with Gershwin scores.

CROSS, Milton, & David EWEN. *Milton Cross' Encyclopedia of the Great*   **99**
Composers and Their Music, 2 vols., rev ed. Garden City, NY:
Doubleday, 1962. 1st ed, 1953.

  Biographical section & program notes for *An American in Paris,
Concerto in F, Porgy and Bess,* & *Rhapsody in Blue.*

CROWNINSHIELD, Frank. "Introduction," *George Gershwin [Catalogue* **100**
of the Gershwin Memorial Exhibition], [2-3].

  Exhibit catalogue for a posthumous exhibit of thirty-nine items
including oil paintings, drawings & water colors, at the Marie Harriman
Gallery, New York City, Dec 18, 1937-Jan 4, 1938.

CROWNINSHIELD, Frank. "Gershwin the Painter," in: *Rhapsody in*   **101**
Blue; the Jubilant Story of George Gershwin and His Music
[Hollywood: Warner Bros, 1945], 11-12.

CROWTHER, Bosley. "Americans in Paris: New Metro Film Affords a   **102**
Fanciful Tour," *The New York Times* CI/34,231 (Oct 14, 1951),
Sec II, 1.

CROWTHER, Bosley. "Fitness of Folk Opera: A Rare Form in Films Is   **103**
Exalted by Goldwyn's 'Porgy and Bess'," *The New York Times*
CVIII/37,045 (June 28, 1959), Sec II, 1.

CROWTHER, Bosley. " 'Porgy and Bess Again': Further Thoughts on a   **104**
Second Look at the Filmed Folk Opera," *The New York Times*
CVIII/37,080 (Aug 2, 1959), Sec II, 1.

CULLAZ, Maurice. "Porgy and Bess," *Jazz Hot* No. 226 (Dec 1966), 7.   **105**
Review of the motion picture.

D

DALY, William. "George Gershwin as Orchestrator," in: Merle   **106**
ARMITAGE, ed, *George Gershwin* (NY: Longmans, Green, 1938),
30-31. Reissued from *The New York Times* LXXXII/27,385
(Jan 15, 1933), Sec X, 6.
Daly's answer to a charge that he orchestrated Gershwin's symphonic
works.

DAMROSCH, Walter. "Gershwin and the Concerto in F," in: Merle   **107**
ARMITAGE, ed, *George Gershwin* (NY: Longmans, Green, 1938),
32-33.

DAMROSCH, Walter. "Gershwin and His Music," in: *Rhapsody in Blue;* **108**
the Jubilant Story of George Gershwin and His Music [Hollywood:
Warner Bros, 1945], 7-8.

DANNENBERG, Peter. "Gelsenkirchen: Nach fünfunddreissig Jahren,   **109**
Gershwin 'Porgy and Bess'," *Opernwelt* XI/11 (Nov 1970), 35-36.
Porgy and Bess after thirty-five years.

DANZ, Louis. "Gershwin and Schoenberg," in: Merle ARMITAGE, ed,   **110**
George Gershwin (NY: Longmans, Green, 1938), 99-101.

DASHIELL, Alan. "Foreword and Discography," in: Isaac GOLDBERG,   **111**
George Gershwin: A Study in American Music (NY: Frederick
Ungar, 1958), xiii-xviii, 357-70.
Discography of long playing records is an addition to the reprint of the
1931 Gershwin biography.

DAVENPORT, Marcia, & Ruth Woodbury SEDGWICK. "Rhapsody in   **112**
Black," *Stage Magazine* XIII/2 (Nov 1935), 31-33.
About *Porgy and Bess.*

DAVID, Hubert W. "Gershwin, The Man We Love," *Melody Maker*   **113**
XXX/1108 (Dec 11, 1954), 8.

"Death of Gershwin," *Time* XXX/3 (July 19, 1937), 37-38.   **114**
Obituary.

"Dick Nash's Word to [the] Worrisome: He's Not Rewriting 'Porgy and   **115**
Bess'," *Variety* CCIX/5 (Jan 1, 1958), 7.
About the screen adaptation of *Porgy and Bess.*

DIETZ, Robert J. *The Operatic Style of Marc Blitzstein in the American*   **116**
"Agit-Prop" Era. Ph.D.Dissertation: University of Iowa, 1970. 358 pp.
UM: 70-15,591. | *Dissertation Abstracts* XXX/3 (Sep 1970), 1307-A.
Several passing references; Blitzstein knew Gershwin.

DOLL, Bill. "Folk Opera Capacity in Washington," *New York Herald*   **117**
Tribune CXII/38,633 (Aug 24, 1952), Sec IV, 1.

DOLL, Bill. "Fan Mail, After Many Years," *Theatre Arts* XLIII/10 (Oct   **118**
1959), 28-32, 84-85.

DONAHUE, Lester. "Gershwin and the Social Scene," in: Merle   **119**
ARMITAGE, ed, *George Gershwin* (NY: Longmans, Green, 1938),
170-77.

DOVE, Ian. " 'Of Thee I Sing' Returned in Musical Style of the '30's."   **120**
Billboard LXXXI/12 (Mar 22, 1969), 14.

DOWNES, Edward. *Adventures in Symphonic Music,* Decorations by   **121**
John O'Hara Cosgrove II. NY: Farrar & Rinehart, 1944. 323 pp.
Program notes for *An American in Paris* & *Rhapsody in Blue.*

DOWNES, Irene, ed. *Olin Downes on Music: A Selection from His*   **122**
Writings during the Half-Century. NY: Simon & Schuster, 1957.
473 pp.
Includes revisions of three reviews. See: Olin DOWNES, Nos. **123,**
128, & **129.**

DOWNES, Olin. "A Concert of Jazz," *The New York Times* LXXIII/   **123**
    24,126 (Feb 13, 1924), 16. Also as: "*Rhapsody in Blue* Introduced
    in a Historic Whiteman Concert," in: Irene DOWNES, ed, *Olin
    Downes on Music: A Selection from His Writings during the Half-
    Century* (NY: Simon & Schuster, 1957), 83-85. Excerpt in: Nicolas
    SLONIMSKY (No. **538**), 385.
    Review of world premiere.

DOWNES, Olin. "A Piano Concerto in the Vernacular to Have Its Day   **124**
    with Damrosch," *The New York Times* LXXV/24,781 (Nov 29,
    1925), Sec VIII, 2.
    Article about the *Concerto in F* prior to its premiere, Dec 3, 1925.

DOWNES, Olin. "Gershwin's New Score Acclaimed," *The New York*   **125**
    Times LXXVIII/25,892 (Dec 14, 1928), 37.
    Review of premiere of *An American in Paris.*

DOWNES, Olin. "George Gershwin Plays His Second Rhapsody for First   **126**
    Time Here with Koussevitsky and Boston Orchestra," *The New York
    Times* LXXXI/27,041 (Feb 6, 1932), 14.

DOWNES, Olin. " 'Porgy and Bess', Native Opera, Opens at the Alvin;   **127**
    Gershwin Work Based on Du Bose Heyward's Play: Exotic Richness
    of Negro Music and Color of Charleston, S.C., Admirably Conveyed
    in Score of Catfish Row Tragedy," *The New York Times* LXXXV/
    28,384 (Oct 11, 1935), 30.

DOWNES, Olin. "When Critics Disagree: Amusing Dramatics and Musical   **128**
    Commentary Upon Gershwin's *Porgy and Bess*," *The New York
    Times* LXXXV/28,395 (Oct 20, 1935), Sec X, 7. Also as: "*Porgy and
    Bess* and the Future of American Opera," in: Irene DOWNES, ed,
    *Olin Downes on Music: A Selection from His Writings during the
    Half-Century* (NY: Simon & Schuster, 1957), 208-11.

DOWNES, Olin. "Hail & Farewell: Career & Position of George Gershwin   **129**
    in American Music," *The New York Times* LXXXVI/29,030 (July
    18, 1937), Sec X, 5. Also as: "Hail and Farewell," in Merle
    ARMITAGE, ed, *George Gershwin* (NY: Longmans, Green, 1938),
    219-24. Also as: "On the Passing of George Gershwin," in: Irene
    DOWNES, ed, *Olin Downes on Music: A Selection from His
    Writings during the Half-Century* (NY: Simon & Schuster, 1957), 232-37.
    Latter entry mistakenly dated August 18, 1937.

DOWNES, Olin. "Gershwin Memorial: Retrospect of Rapid Rise of   **130**
Composer and the Development of His Art," *The New York Times*
LXXXVII/29,387 (July 10, 1938), Sec IX, 5.

DOWNES, Olin. " 'Porgy' Fantasy: R[obert] R[ussell] Bennett Makes   **131**
Symphonic Work from Gershwin Opera," *The New York Times*
XCII/30,976 (Nov 15, 1942), Sec VIII, 7.

DOWNES, Olin. Papers. See: University of Georgia, Athens, No. **608**.

"Drama: Dissenting Opinion," *The Nation* CXLI/3669 (Oct 30, 1935),   **132**
518-19.
  About *Porgy and Bess*.

"Dubbing In the Voices, Also a Big Production," *Life* XLVI/24 (June 15, **133**
1954), 79-82.
  Discusses the dubbing of the singing voices in the film *Porgy and Bess*.

D[ÜRR], A[lfred]. "In Memoriam: George Gershwin (1898-1937),"   **134**
Musica XI/1 (Jan 1957), 38-39.
  German version of an article in *Harper's Magazine*.

DUKE, Vernon. "Gershwin, Schillinger, and Dukelsky—Some   **135**
Reminiscences," *The Musical Quarterly* XXXIII/1 (Jan 1947), 102-15.
  Duke discusses his and Gershwin's studies with Schillinger.

DUKE, Vernon. *Passport to Paris*. Boston: Little, Brown, 1955. 502 pp. **136**
  Reminiscences about George and Ira Gershwin are included in this
  autobiography.

DUKE, Vernon. *Listen Here*. NY: I. Obolensky, 1963. 406 pp.   **137**
  A vitriolic assessment of music and musicians.

DUKELSKY, Vladimir. See: Vernon DUKE, Nos. **135-37**.

DUNCAN, Todd. "Memoirs of George Gershwin," in: Merle   **138**
ARMITAGE, ed, *George Gershwin* (NY: Longmans, Green, 1938),
58-64.

*DURHAM, Frank. *DuBose Heyward, the Man Who Wrote Porgy*.   **139**
Columbia, SC: University of South Carolina Press, 1954. 152 pp.

E

ECKSTEIN, Pavel. "Gershwinuv 'Porgy a Bess'," *Hudebni Rozhledy*   **140**
XXIV/4 (Apr 1971), 155.
Review of *Porgy and Bess* in Brno.

EDENS, Roger. "Labor Pains," *Film and TV Music* XVI/3 (Spring   **141**
1957), 18-20.
Discusses the motion picture *Funny Face*.

EDWARDS, Arthur C., & W. Thomas MARROCCO. *Music in the*   **142**
United States (Dubuque, Ia: Wm. C. Brown, 1968), 105-6, 107,
117, 154.
Compact survey in a few paragraphs.

EELLS, George. *The Life That Late He Led: A Biography of Cole*   **143**
Porter. NY: G. P. Putnam's; London: W. H. Allen, 1967. 383 pp.

ELISOFON, Eliot. See: Arthur KNIGHT, No. **331**.

ELLSWORTH, Ray. "Americans in Microgroove: Part II," *High Fidelity* **144**
VI/8 (Aug 1956), 60-66.
Discusses recordings of Gershwin's works.

ELLSWORTH, Ray. "The RCA Victor 'Porgy and Bess'," *The American* **145**
Record Guide XXX/3 (Nov 1963), 196-99.
Record review.

E[NGEL], C[arl]. "Views and Reviews," *The Musical Quarterly* XII/2   **146**
(Apr 1926), 299-314.
Discusses Gershwin's *Concerto in F*.

E[NGEL], C[arl]. "Views and Reviews," *The Musical Quarterly* XVIII/4 **147**
(Oct 1932), 646-51.
A review of *George Gershwin's Song-Book*.

"Escenas del estreno de la opera Porgy and Bess de George Gershwin en   **148**
la Staatsoper de Viena," *Boletin de Musica y Artes Visuales, Pan
American Union* Nos. 36-37 (Feb-Mar 1953), 22-25.
Reviews 1952 Vienna performance of *Porgy and Bess*.

EWEN, David. "A New Gilbert and Sullivan on Broadway," *The*   **149**
American Hebrew CXXI/17 (Sep 2, 1927), 517, 522-30.
About George Gershwin & George S. Kaufman.

EWEN, David. "A Master of Symponic Jazz," *The Jewish Tribune*   **150**
XCI/15 (Oct 7, 1927), 16.

EWEN, David. "New Harmonists," *The American Hebrew* CXXIII/16   **151**
(Aug 24, 1928), 435, 441.
About Louis Gruenberg, Aaron Copland, Marion Bauer & George
Gershwin.

EWEN, David. "The King of Tin-Pan Alley," *The Jewish Tribune* XCIV/ **152**
7 (Feb 15, 1929), 2, 11.

EWEN, David. "George Gershwin, America's Musical Hope," *Gamut*   **153**
[New York] II/5 (Nov 1929), 30-31.

EWEN, David, ed. *Composers of Today* (NY: H. W. Wilson, 1934), 85-86. **154**

EWEN, David. *Twentieth Century Composers.* NY: Thomas Y. Crowell, **155**
1937. 309 pp.

EWEN, David. "Farewell to George Gershwin," in: Merle ARMITAGE, **156**
ed, *George Gershwin* (NY: Longmans, Green, 1938), 203-8.

EWEN, David. *The Story of George Gershwin,* illustrated by Graham **157**
Bernbach. NY: Henry Holt, 1943. 211 pp. German translation by
Gunther Martin, with a foreward by Friedrich Gulda, as: *George
Gershwin: Leben und Werk.* Zürich: Amalthea-Verlag, 1954. 155 pp.
Dutch translation as: *George Gershwin.* Haarlem: Gottmer, 1958.
244 pp.

EWEN, David. *Men of Popular Music.* Chicago/NY: Ziff-Davis, 1944. **158**
213 pp.

EWEN, David. "The Stature of George Gershwin," *The American*   **159**
Mercury LXX/318 (June 1950), 716-24.

EWEN, David, ed. *The Book of Modern Composers,* 2nd ed, rev &   **160**
enlarged. NY: A. A. Knopf, 1950. 586 pp. 1st ed, 1942.

Contains a brief biography, comments by Isaac Goldberg, an excerpt
from an article by Gershwin discussing his aesthetic theories, and an
essay by John Tasker Howard.

EWEN, David. "The Mighty Five of American Popular Music," *Theatre*   **161**
Arts XXXV/12 (Dec 1951), 42, 74-76.

EWEN, David. *Ewen's Musical Masterworks: The Encyclopedia of*   **162**
Musical Masterpieces, 2nd ed. NY: Arco, 1954. 1st ed, 1944.

Program notes for *An American in Paris, Concerto in F & Rhapsody
in Blue.*

EWEN, David. *George Gershwin: Leben und Werk* (1954). See: David
EWEN, *The Story of George Gershwin,* No. **157**.

EWEN, David. "Gershwin Would be Surprised," *Harper's Magazine*   **163**
CCX/1260 (May 1955), 68-70.

About the growth of Gershwin's fame since his death.

EWEN, David. "A Wartime 'Porgy'," *The New York Times* CV/35,687   **164**
(Oct 9, 1955), Sec II, 1, 3.

First European performance in 1943 in Nazi-occupied Denmark of
Porgy and Bess.

EWEN, David. *A Journey to Greatness.* NY: Henry Holt; London: **165**
W. H. Allen, 1956. 384 pp.

EWEN, David. *George Gershwin* (1958). See: David EWEN, *The Story
of George Gershwin,* No. **157**.

EWEN, David, ed. *The Complete Book of 20th Century Music,* new &   **166**
rev ed. Englewood Cliffs, NJ: Prentice-Hall, 1959. 1st ed, 1952.

Program notes for *An American in Paris, Concerto in F & Rhapsody
in Blue.*

EWEN, David. *The Story of America's Musical Theatre* (Philadelphia: **167**
Chilton, 1961), 89-93, 112-20, 141-47, 167-68, *et al.*

EWEN, David. *The Life and Death of Tin Pan Alley.* NY: Funk &   **168**
Wagnalls, 1964.

EWEN, David. "There'll Always Be a Gershwin," *Variety* CCXLI/7   **169**
(Jan 5, 1966), 207.

EWEN, David. *George Gershwin: His Journey to Greatness.* Englewood   **170**
Cliffs, NJ: Prentice-Hall, 1970. 354 pp.

A revised, updated version of *A Journey to Greatness* (See: No. **165**),
but with many factual errors retained and without the earlier book's
discography and bibliography. RILM[70] 842.

EWEN, David. "Miami: A Festival of George Gershwin," *High Fidelity/*   **171**
Musical America XXI/1 (Jan 1971), MA 24-25+.

Works discussed include: *In a Mandarin's Orchid Garden, Lullaby,
135th Street & Promenade.*

EWEN, David, & Milton CROSS. See: Milton CROSS, No. **99**.

"Exhibit of Gershwiniana at N.Y.C. Museum Pulls Int'l Show Biz Crowd," **172**
Variety CCL/12 (May 8, 1968), 241+.

F

FABRICANT, Noah D., M.D. "George Gershwin's Fatal Headache,"   **173**
The Eye, Ear, Nose and Throat Monthly XXXVII/5 (May 1958),
332-34.

A doctor's assessment of Gershwin's fatal illness.

FIECHTNER, Helmut A. "Gershwin's 'Porgy and Bess'," *Musica* XX/1   **174**
(Jan 1966), 23-24.

Review of the Vienna production.

"Filming 'Rhapsody in Blue'," in: *Rhapsody in Blue; the Jubilant Story* **175**
of George Gershwin and His Music [Hollywood: Warner Bros,
1945], 19-20.

"First Gershwin Festival," *Music Educators Journal* LVII/1 (Sep 1970),   **176**
79.

Notice of a Gershwin festival at the University of Miami.

"First World Festival—Gershwin Serious Music, Miami," *Pan Pipes of*   **177**
Sigma Alpha Iota LXIII/2 (Jan 1971), 35.

FISK UNIVERSITY. Nashville. Library. *Selected Items from the*   **178**
   George Gershwin Memorial Collection of Music and Musical Literature
   Founded by Carl Van Vechten. Nashville: Fisk University, 1947. 32 pp.

   Introduction by Arna Bontemps, Fisk University Librarian; twelve
   letters, dozens of books & scores, manuscripts, photographs, & discs.
   Several items of Gershwin interest including scores & manuscript
   fragments.

"Folk Opera," *Time* XXVI/17 (Oct 21, 1935), 48.   **179**

FOSSUM, Knut. "Norway: Romantic 'Porgy'," *Opera* XIX/1 (Jan   **180**
   1968), 62-63.

   Review of *Porgy and Bess* at the Norwegian Opera.

FRANKENSTEIN. Alfred. "An American in Paris," *San Francisco*   **181**
   Symphony Orchestra [Program] (Nov 2, 1951), 93. Also in:
   Ibid., (Nov 18, 1954), 63+.

FRANKENSTEIN, Alfred. *A Modern Guide to Symphonic Music* (NY: **182**
   Meredith Press, 1966), 244-46.

   Program notes for *Concerto in F.* Originally appeared in a *San*
   Francisco Symphony Orchestra Program.

"Freed Sets Gershwin Film," *Down Beat* XXVI/11 (May 28, 1949), 14.   **183**

FREEDLEY, Vinton. "'Porgy' and Always the Best," *The Saturday*   **184**
   Review XLI/42 (Oct 18, 1958), 14.

   Review of *The Gershwin Years* by Jablonski & Stewart (See: No. **304**).

FRIEDRICH, Götz. "Zwanzig Notizen zu einer Aufführungskonzeption   **185**
   von *Porgy and Bess*," *Jahrbuch der Komischen Oper Berlin* IX
   (1969), 153-62. RILM69 1292.

FUNKE, Lewis. "News and Gossip of the Rialto: 'Porgy and Bess' Loses **186**
   Official Support," *The New York Times* CV/35,680 (Oct 2, 1955),
   Sec II, 1.

G

GALLOWAY, Kay Swift. See: Kay SWIFT, No. **566**.

GARLAND, Robert. "Negroes are Critical of 'Porgy and Bess'," *New*   **187**
    York World Telegram LXVIII/167 (Jan 16, 1936), 14.

*GARSON, Edith. "Supplements," in: Isaac GOLDBERG, *George*   **188**
    Gershwin; A Study in American Music (NY: Frederick Ungar, 1958),
    297-356.

    Garson adds six chapters, primarily of an updating sort, to the
    original Goldberg book of 1931 (See: No. **234**).

*GAUTHIER, Eva. "Personal Appreciation," in: Merle ARMITAGE, ed,   **189**
    George Gershwin (NY: Longmans, Green, 1938), 193-202.

GAUTHIER, Eva. "The Roaring Twenties," *Musical Courier* CLI/3 (Feb   **190**
    1, 1955), 42-44.

    Miss Gauthier tells of Gershwin's first meeting with Ravel at a party
    in her home.

GAUTHIER, Eva. See: Henry W. LEVINGER, No. **364**.

"George Gershwin," *Etude* LV/9 (Sep 1937), 558.   **191**
    Obituary.

"George Gershwin," in: *The ASCAP Biographical Dictionary of*   **192**
    Composers, Authors and Publishers, 1966 ed, compiled and edited by
    The Lynn Farnol Group, Inc. (NY: ASCAP, 1966), 256-57.

    Lists shows, songs, etc.

"George Gershwin [1898-1937]," *Journal Musical Français* No. 155   **193**
    (Mar 1967), 41-42.

Georgia, University of. See: UNIVERSITY OF GEORGIA, No. **608**.

"German Orchestra (U.S. Soloists) in First West German Tour with All-   **194**
    Gershwin Program," *Variety* CXCIX/13 (Aug 31, 1955), 2+.

GERSHWIN, Alan. "I am George Gershwin's Illegitimate Son,"   **195**
    Confidential VI/6 (Feb 1959), 10-13, 45-46.

"Gershwin Benefit Concert by Whiteman Tonight," *New York Herald*   **196**
     Tribune CXIV/39,534 (Feb 12, 1955), 8.

"Gershwin Concert Orchestra Filling 100 Dates on Tour," *Musical*   **197**
     Courier CXLVII/4 (Feb 15, 1953), 37.

"Gershwin Everywhere," *Time* XLVI/2 (July 9, 1945), 67.   **198**

"Gershwin Festival Scheduled in October," *Music Clubs Magazine* L/1   **199**
     (Autumn 1970), 19.

"Gershwin 50th Anniversary in ASCAP Celebrated in Miami Festival,"   **200**
     ASCAP Today V/1 (Mar 1971), 20.

"Gershwin im Sinfoniekonzert der Stuttgarter Philharmoniker," *Das*   **201**
     Orchester XII/9 (Sep 1964), 295-96.

"Gershwin Memorabilia," *Variety* CCXLVII/4 (June 14, 1967), 50.   **202**
     Tells of the Gershwin memorabilia to be housed in The Museum of
     the City of New York.

"Gershwin Memorials," *Time* XXXII/4 (July 25, 1938), 33-34.   **203**

"Gershwin Orchestra Tours 74 Cities," *Musical America* LXXIV/2 (Jan   **204**
     15, 1954), 4.

"Gershwin Rhapsody Thirty Years Old," *Music Dealer* VIII/2 (Feb   **205**
     1954), 11.

"Gershwin Service Here on Thursday," *The New York Times* LXXXVI/   **206**
     29,925 (July 13, 1937), 20.

"Gershwin: Talented Composer Gave *Porgy* Life and Rhythm," *News-*   **207**
     Week VI/15 (Oct 12, 1935), 22.

"Gershwin." See: "Gershwins" (No. **226**), "Gershwin's" (Nos. **225** &
     227; Nos. **191-93**), & Ira (Nos. **288-89**).

GERSHWIN, George. "Does Jazz Belong to Art?" *Second Line* XIV   **208**
     (Sep-Oct 1965), 120-23. Reprinted from *Singing* I/7 (July 1926),
     13-14.

GERSHWIN, George. "Mr. Gershwin Replies to Mr. Kramer," *Singing*   **209**
I/10 (Oct 1926), 17-18.

Gershwin answers a charge by A. Walter Kramer in *Singing* (See:
No. **348**) that he did not orchestrate the *Concerto in F*.

*GERSHWIN, George. "The Composer and the Machine Age," in: Merle   **210**
ARMITAGE, ed, *George Gershwin* (NY: Longmans, Green, 1938),
225-30. Originally appeared in: Oliver SAYLER, ed, *Revolt in the
Arts.* NY: Brentano's, 1930. 351 pp. [Rights turned over to Coward-
McCann, 1933.] Also in: Gilbert CHASE, ed, *The American
Composer Speaks: A Historical Anthology, 1770-1965* (Baton Rouge,
La: Louisiana State University Press, 1966), 139-45 (Includes an
introduction by Gilbert Chase; RILM[67] 76) Also, with deletions, in:
Sam MORGENSTERN, ed, *Composers on Music: An Anthology of
Composers' Writings from Palestrina to Copland* (NY: Pantheon,
1956), 510-13 (Includes an introduction by Sam Morgenstern).

GERSHWIN, George. "Introduction," in: Isaac GOLDBERG, *Tin Pan*   **211**
Alley: A Chronicle of the American Popular Music Racket (NY: John
Day, 1930), vii-xi. Reprint, with supplement by Edward Jablonski,
as: *Tin Pan Alley: A Chronicle of American Popular Music* (NY:
Frederick Ungar, 1961).

Gershwin discusses his composing habits.

*GERSHWIN, George. "The Relation of Jazz to American Music," in: **212**
Henry COWELL, ed, *American Composers on American Music*
(Palo Alto: Stanford University Press, 1933; reprint, NY: Frederick
Ungar, 1962), 186-87. Other Gershwin citations, 8, 139, 207. Also
in: Elie SIEGMEISTER, ed, *The Music Lover's Handbook* (NY:
William Morrow, 1943), 728-29.

*GERSHWIN, George. "Rhapsody in Catfish Row: Mr. Gershwin Tells the **213**
Origin and Scheme for His Music in That New Folk Opera Called
'Porgy and Bess'," *The New York Times* LXXXV/28,395 (Oct 20,
1935), Sec X, 102. Also as: "Rhapsody in Catfish Row," in: Merle
ARMITAGE, ed, *George Gershwin* (NY: Longmans, Green, 1938),
72-77.

*GERSHWIN, Ira. "My Brother," in: Merle ARMITAGE, ed, *George*   **214**
Gershwin (NY: Longmans, Green, 1938), 16-23. Also in: Merle
ARMITAGE, *George Gershwin: Man and Legend* (NY: Duell, Sloan,
& Pearce, 1958), 11-18.

GERSHWIN, Ira. "Gershwin on Gershwin," *News-Week* XXIV/17   **215**
(Oct 23, 1944), 14.

Ira Gershwin voices objections to allegations that his brother had
started studying with Schillinger because his creative well had run dry.

GERSHWIN, Ira. "Twenty Years After," *The New Yorker* XXVIII/13   **216**
(May 17, 1952), 26-27.

GERSHWIN, Ira. "[New York Is a Great Place to Be]...But I Wouldn't **217**
Want to Live There," *The Saturday Review* XLI/42 (Oct 18, 1958),
27, 48. (Leonard Lyons wrote first portion. See: No. **380**).

*GERSHWIN, Ira. *Lyrics on Several Occasions; a Selection of Stage &*   . **218**
*Screen Lyrics Written for Sundry Situations; and Now Arranged in
Arbitrary Categories. To Which Have Been Added Many Informative
Annotations & Disquisitions on Their Why & Wherefore, Their
Whom-For, Their How; and Matters Associative.* NY: A.A. Knopf,
1959. 362 pp.

GERSHWIN, Ira. "Which Came First?" *The Saturday Review* XLII/35   **219**
(Aug 29, 1959), 31-33, 45.

Excerpts from his *Lyrics on Several Occasions.*

GERSHWIN, Ira. "Frederick Lowe: Four Scores (and Seven Years Ago)," **220**
The New York Times CIX/37,318 (Mar 27, 1960), Sec II, 5.

GERSHWIN, Ira. "That Inevitable Question: Which Comes First?"   **221**
Variety CCXXV/7 (Jan 10, 1962), 187.

Comments on whether words or music come first in writing popular songs.

GERSHWIN, Ira. "Euterpe and the Lucky Lyricist," *Variety* CCXXXIII/ **222**
7 (Jan 8, 1964), 198.

GERSHWIN, Ira. [Diary].   **223**

Provides daily account of period of *Porgy and Bess* premiere in
Moscow (1956).

GERSHWIN, Ira. [Archive of materials includes diary, letters,   **224**
memorabilia, photographs].

"Gershwin's American Opera Puts Audience on Its Feet," *News-Week* **225**
VI/16 (Oct 19, 1935), 23-24.

"Gershwins Honored," *Variety* CCXLIII/2 (June 1, 1966), 45.   **226**

" 'Gershwin's Music Subversive' Says Senator McCarthy," *Melody Maker* **227**
XXIX/1031 (June 13, 1953), 12.

GILDER, Rosamond. "Places and People: Broadway in Review," **228**
Theatre Arts XXVI/4 (Apr 1942), 219-26.
Porgy and Bess discussed on pp. 219-20.

GILMAN, Lawrence. "Paul Whiteman and the Palais Royalists Extend **229**
Their Kingdom; Jazz at Aeolian Hall," *New York Tribune* LXXXIII/
28,213 (Feb 17, 1924), 9. Excerpt in: Nicolas SLONIMSKY,
Nos. **536** & **538**.

GILMAN, Lawrence. "George Gershwin's New Opera, Porgy and Bess, **230**
Produced by the Theatre Guild," *New York Herald Tribune*
XCV/32,471 (Oct 11, 1935). See: Nicolas SLONIMSKY, No. **536**.

GOLDBERG, Isaac. "George Gershwin and Jazz: A Critical Analysis of **231**
a Modern Composer," *Theatre Guild Magazine* VII/6 (Mar 1930),
15-19, 55.
Discusses *Strike Up the Band*. Incorporated into the author's 1931
biography, No. **234**.

GOLDBERG, Isaac. "Jazzo-Analysis," *Disques* [Philadelphia] I/9 (Nov **232**
1930), 394-98.

*GOLDBERG, Isaac. *Tin Pan Alley; A Chronicle of the American Popular* **233**
Music Racket, with an introduction by George Gershwin. NY: John
Day, 1930. 341 pp. Reprint, with a supplement by Edward
Jablonski, as: *Tin Pan Alley; A Chronicle of American Popular Music*
(NY: Frederick Ungar, 1961). 371 pp.

GOLDBERG, Isaac. *George Gershwin: A Study in American Music.* **234**
NY: Simon & Schuster, 1931. 305 pp. Reprint edition supplemented
by Edith Garson, with a foreward and discography by Alan Dashiell.
NY: Frederick Ungar, 1958. 387 pp.
First biography, written when Gershwin was thirty-three years old.
Quotes from many reviews, 1924-30.

GOLDBERG, Isaac. "Music by Gershwin," *Ladies Home Journal*   **235**
   XLVIII/2 (Feb 1931), 12-13; XLVIII/3 (Mar 1931), 20+; XLVIII/
   4 (Apr 1931), 25+.
   These articles were incorporated into Goldberg's biography, No. **234**.

GOLDBERG, Isaac. "Gebrüder Gershwin," *Vanity Fair* XXXVIII/4   **236**
   (June 1932), 46-47, 62.

GOLDBERG, Isaac. "American Operetta Comes of Age; Annotations   **237**
   Upon *Of Thee I Sing* and Its Merry Makers," *Disques* [Philadelphia]
   III/1 (Mar 1932), 7-12.

GOLDBERG, Isaac. "Music in the Air: Let Us Eat Cake," *The Musical*   **238**
   Record I/6 (Nov 1933), 216-19.
   Favorable comments about *Let 'Em Eat Cake*.

GOLDBERG, Isaac. "Music in the Air: Schönberg–Gershwin–A New   **239**
   Phonographic Venture," *The Musical Record* I/9 (Feb 1934),
   326-29.
   Touches on Gershwin's tour with the Reisman orchestra.

GOLDBERG, Isaac. "Score by George Gershwin," *Stage Magazine*   **240**
   XIII/3 (Dec 1935), 37-38.
   Praises *Porgy and Bess*.

GOLDBERG, Isaac. "What's Jewish in Gershwin's Music," *B'nai B'rith*   **241**
   Magazine L/7 (Apr 1936), 226-27, 247.
   Goldberg alludes to Jewish elements in Gershwin's music.

GOLDBERG, Isaac. "In Memoriam: George Gershwin," *B'nai B'rith*   **242**
   Magazine LII/1 (Aug-Sep 1937), 8-9, 26.

*GOLDBERG, Isaac. "Homage to a Friend," in: Merle ARMITAGE, ed,   **243**
   George Gershwin (NY: Longmans, Green, 1938), 161-67.

GOLDBERG, Isaac. "Personal Note," in: David EWEN, ed, *The Book of* **244**
   Modern Composers, 2nd ed rev & enlarged. NY: A. A. Knopf,
   1950. 586 pp. 1st ed, 1942.

GOTTFRIED, Martin. "Why Is Broadway Music So Bad?" *Music News*   **245**
   (Jan 1971), 4-5.

GOULD, Jack. "Television in Review: '135th Street', Written by   **246**
      Gershwin at 22, Is Offered by 'Omnibus' in Local Premiere,"
      The New York Times CII/34,764 (Mar 30, 1953), 18.

GRABBE, Paul. *The Story of One Hundred Symphonic Favorites.* NY: **247**
      Grosset & Dunlap, 1940. 300 pp.
      Program notes for *Concerto in F.*

GRAF, Max. " 'Porgy and Bess' Begins European Tour in Vienna,"   **248**
      Musical America LXXII/12 (Oct 1952), 9.

"The Great Songwriters and Records of Their Great Songs," *Billboard*   **249**
      LXII/40 (Oct 7, 1950), supplement, 79-81.

GREEN, Abel. "[George and Ira] Gershwin Song Book," *Variety*   **250**
      CCXX/6 (Oct 5, 1960), 59.

GREEN, Benny. "Gershwin's *Porgy and Bess,*" *Music and Musicians*   **251**
      XI/2 (Oct 1962), 22-23.

GREEN, Stanley. "Catfish Row in a 'Near Original'," *HiFi Review* III/2   **252**
      (Aug 1959), 40.
      Review of the soundtrack of the film *Porgy and Bess.*

GREEN, Stanley. "A Songwriter by Any Other Name. . . ," *Variety*   **253**
      CCXXXIII/7 (Jan 8, 1964), 195.

GREEN, Stanley. *Ring Bells! Sing Songs! Broadway Musicals of the*   **254**
      1930's. New Rochelle, NY: Arlington House, 1971. 385 pp.
      Includes information about Gershwin's scores for Broadway during
      the thirties from *Strike Up the Band* (1930) onward.

*GREEN, Stanley. *The World of Musical Comedy,* with a foreword by   **254a**
      Deems Taylor, 2nd ed, rev & enlarged. South Brunswick, NJ:
      A. S. Barnes, 1968. 541 pp. 1st ed, 1960.
      Reviews the development of musical comedy in America.

GRIGOŘEV, Lev Grigořevič, & Jakov Michajlovič PLATEK. *Džordž*   **255**
      Gershvin. Moscow: Gos. Muz. Izd, 1956. 43 pp.

GROFÉ, Ferde. "George Gershwin's Influence," in: Merle ARMITAGE,   **256**
      ed, *George Gershwin* (NY: Longmans, Green, 1938), 27-29.

GROVE'S DICTIONARY. See: Eric BLOM, No. **44**.

GRUNFELD, Fred. "The Great American Opera," *Opera News* XXIV/   **257**
20 (Mar 19, 1960), 6-9.
About *Porgy and Bess.*

GUADAGNINO, Luigi. "Conclusioni su 'Porgy and Bess'," *La Scala*   **258**
No. 89 (Apr 1957), 64-68. French, English & German summaries,
103-4.

H

H., C. "Gershwin's Music Jams the Stadium," *The New York Times*   **259**
XCVIII/33,403 (July 8, 1949), 14.

HAGGIN, Bernard H. "Gershwin and Our Music," *The Nation* CXXXV/ **260**
3509 (Oct 5, 1932), 308-9.

HAGGIN, Bernard H. "Music," *The Nation* CLXI/5 (Aug 4, 1945), 115. **261**

HAINES, Charles. "George Gershwin ovvero del musicista come eroe,"   **262**
L'Approdo musicale I/4 (Oct-Dec 1958), 3-23.

HALE, Philip. "Rhapsody, No. 2, for Orchestra," *Boston Symphony*   **263**
Orchestra Programmes LI/14 (Jan 29-30, 1932), 838-54.
Program notes, with interesting biographical information & quotes
from letters, for world premiere, Gershwin as soloist.

HAMMERSTEIN, Oscar. "Gershwin," *The Music Journal* VIII/4 (Apr   **264**
1955), 21.

HAMMERSTEIN, Oscar, II. "To George Gershwin," in: Merle   **265**
ARMITAGE, ed, *George Gershwin* (NY: Longmans, Green, 1938),
1-4. Reissued from *The George Gershwin Memorial Concert
Programme* (Hollywood Bowl, Sep 6, 1937).

HANDY, William C. *Blues.* NY: A & C Boni, 1926. 180 pp.   **266**

HANGEN, Welles. " 'Porgy and Bess' in the USSR," *The New York*   **267**
Times CV/35,785 (Jan 15, 1956), Sec II, 3.

HANSON, Howard. "Flowering of American Music," *The Saturday*   **268**
    Review of Literature XXXII/32 (Aug 6, 1949), 157-64.
    Deals with Gershwin on page 160.

HANSON, John Robert. *Macroforms in Selected Twentieth-Century*   **269**
    Piano Concertos. Ph.D. Dissertation: Eastman, University of
    Rochester, 1969. 404 pp. UM:70-10, 575. *Dissertation Abstracts*
    XXX/12 (June 1970), 5469-A.
    Gershwin's piano works with orchestra compared with thirty three
    other concerti. RILM[69] 4152.

HARRIS, Sam H. "Gershwin and Gold," in: Merle ARMITAGE, ed,   **270**
    George Gershwin (NY: Longmans, Green, 1938), 168-69.

HELM, Everett. "To Talk of Many Things," *Musical America* LXXXII/7 **271**
    (July 1962), 46.

HENRY-JACQUES. See: Henry- JACQUES, No. **306**.

HEYWARD, Dorothy (Hartzell). "Porgy's Goat," *Harper's Magazine*   **272**
    CCXV/1291 (Dec 1957), 37-41.

*HEYWARD, Dorothy & DuBose. *Porgy.* NY: Doubleday, Page, 1927.   **273**
    203 pp.
    Play version of 1925 novel.

*HEYWARD, DuBose. *Porgy.* NY: Doran, 1925. 196 pp.   **274**

HEYWARD, DuBose. "Porgy and Bess Return on Wings of Song," in: **275**
    Merle ARMITAGE, ed, *George Gershwin* (NY: Longmans, Green,
    1938), 34-42. Reprinted from *Stage Magazine* XIII/1 (Oct 1935),
    25-28.
    Heyward discusses his collaboration with Gershwin on *Porgy and Bess.*

HILL, Richard S. "Music," *The Library of Congress Quarterly Journal*   **276**
    of Current Acquisitions XI/1 (Nov 1953), 15-26.
    Brief mention (p. 15) of Mrs. Rose Gershwin's bequest of scores &
    sketches of orchestral works.

HITCHCOCK, Hugh Wiley. *Music in the United States: A Historical*   **277**
    Introduction (Englewood Cliffs, NJ: Prentice-Hall, 1969), 178,
    187-88, 218-19, 252.

HOGARTH, Basil. "Strange Case of George Gershwin," *The Chesterian*   **278**
  XV [= No. 115] (May-June 1934), 130-36.

HOHLWEG, Rudolf. "Strassburg: Besessen vom Spiel, Gershwin 'Porgy   **279**
  and Bess'," *Opernwelt* X/3 (Mar 1969), 44-45.
  Review of *Porgy and Bess.*

" 'Homage to Gershwin', Transcribed for Violin by Efrem Zimbalist,"   **280**
  Repertoire I/1 (Jan 1952), 172.
  Review of Zimbalist's transcription of the work published by Harms,
  1951.

HOWARD, John Tasker. *Our American Music: A Comprehensive History*   **281**
  from 1620 to the Present, 4th ed (NY: Thomas Y. Crowell, 1965),
  424-29, 797-98, *et al.* 1st ed, 1931.
  Compact but useful survey; numerous other collective citations on
  Gershwin.

HOWARD, John Tasker. "George Gershwin," in: Oscar THOMPSON,   **282**
  The International Cyclopedia of Music and Musicians, 4th ed
  (NY: Dodd, Mead, 1964), 785-86. 1st ed, 1937.

HOWARD, John Tasker. *Our Contemporary Composers* (NY: Thomas   **283**
  Y. Crowell, 1941), 306-11, *et al.* Also as: "George Gershwin," in:
  Elie SIEGMEISTER, ed, *The Music Lover's Handbook* (NY: William
  Morrow, 1943), 453-57.
  Includes a sketch of the composer and his music.

HOWARD, John Tasker. *This Modern Music: A Guide for the*   **284**
  Bewildered Listener (NY: Thomas Y. Crowell, 1942), 123, 185,
  190-91.

HOWARD, John Tasker. "George Gershwin," in: David EWEN, ed, *The*   **285**
  Book of Modern Composers, 2nd ed rev & enlarged. NY: A. A.
  Knopf, 1950. 886 pp. 1st ed (1943), 488-92.

HOWARD, John Tasker. & George Kent BELLOWS. "George Gershwin   **286**
  Symbolizes the Growth of Jazz," in their: *A Short History of*
  Music in America (NY: Thomas Y. Crowell, 1957), 246-50, *et al.*
  Numerous citations, with special remarks on *Of Thee I Sing, Porgy*
  and Bess, & *Rhapsody in Blue.*

I

"Inside Stuff—Music," *Variety* CCII/5 (Apr 4, 1956), 49.   **287**
> Concerning Gershwin's debt to Joseph Schillinger.

"Ira Gershwin Donates $1,500 Annually to School Named for Brother   **288**
George," *Variety* CCXXXVI/5 (Sep 23, 1964), 83.
> An announcement that Ira Gershwin would contribute that amount
> yearly, to be divided among ten gifted students at Brooklyn's George
> Gershwin Junior High School.

"Ira Gershwin Opposes Filming 'Porgy' Now," *Variety* CCI/10 (Feb 8,   **289**
1956), 1+.

"Iron Curtain 'Agents' $1,000,000 Pic Deal on Gershwin's 'Porgy',"   **290**
Variety CCII/2 (Mar 14, 1956), 1+.

ISAACS, Edith J. R. "See America First: Broadway in Review,"   **291**
Theatre Arts Monthly XIX/12 (Dec 1935), 888-902.
> Review of *Porgy and Bess,* pp. 893-94.

ISRAEL, Robert A. "Great Man of Music," *Southwestern Musician*   **292**
XIX/5 (Jan 1953), 13+.
> Tribute to Gershwin.

ITURBI, José. "Gershwin Abroad," in: *Rhapsody in Blue; the Jubilant*   **293**
Story of George Gershwin and His Music [Hollywood: Warner Bros,
1945], 9-10.

J

JABLONSKI, Edward. "Gershwin After 20 Years," *Hi-Fi Music at Home* **294**
III/3 (July-Aug 1956), 22-23, 52, 54, 56-58.
> An evaluation of the composer twenty years after his death; includes
> discography.

J[ABLONSKI], E[dward]. "Unlikely Corners," *The American Record*   **295**
Guide XXIII/8 (May 1957), 131.
> Includes record review of soundtrack from film, *Funny Face* (Verve
> MGV-15001).

J[ABLONSKI], E[dward]. "Unlikely Corners," *The American Record*   **296**
Guide XXIV/1 (Sep 1957), 34-35.

Record reviews of Gershwin albums by Sarah Vaughan and Chris Connor.

JABLONSKI. Edward. "The American Musical," *Hi-Fi Music at Home*   **297**
V/7 (Oct 1958), 43-55.

Brief history of the American musical (see particularly pp. 47-48); includes Gershwin discography.

JABLONSKI, Edward. "An Almost Completely New Work: Gershwin's   **298**
Own Suite from 'Porgy and Bess'," *The American Record Guide* XXV/12 (Aug 1959), 848-49.

Record review of the suite.

JABLONSKI, Edward. "Gershwin Plays Gershwin—Enjoy, Enjoy," *The*   **299**
American Record Guide XXVIII/5 (Jan 1962), 365.

Review of a recording (Distinguished Records 107) of Gershwin at the piano, taken from piano rolls.

JABLONSKI, Edward. "Gershwin on Music," *Musical America*   **300**
LXXXIII/7 (July 1962), 32-35.

Gershwin is quoted speaking about himself and his work.

JABLONSKI, Edward. "Photo by George Gershwin: A Portfolio of   **301**
Originals," *The American Record Guide* XXVIII/11 (July 1962), 844-48.

Some photos by Gershwin of friends and associates.

JABLONSKI, Edward. "Ira Gershwin—Reluctant Celebrity," *Listen*   **302**
I/3 (Mar-Apr 1964), 14-15.

JABLONSKI, Edward. "George Gershwin," *HiFi/Stereo Review* XVIII/   **303**
5 (May 1967), 49-61.

*JABLONSKI, Edward, & Lawrence D. STEWART. *The Gershwin Years,*   **304**
with an introduction by Carl Van Vechten. Garden City, NY: Doubleday, 1973. 416 pp. 1st ed, 1958. For a review of 1st ed, see: Vinton FREEDLEY, No. **184**.

A revised, updated version of the 1958 book.

JACOBI, Frederick. "The Future of Gershwin," *Modern Music* XV/1 **305**
(Nov-Dec 1937), 3-7.
Critical evaluation of the composer.

JACQUES, Henry-. "Deux oeuvres de George Gershwin," *Disques* V **306**
[=No. 45] (Feb 1952), 111.
Record reviews of *An American in Paris & Rhapsody in Blue.*

JANIS, Harriet. See: Rudi BLESH, No. **43**.

"Jazz Concerto," *The Outlook* CXLI/16 (Dec 16, 1925), 582-83. **307**
About *Concerto in F.*

"Jazzed Homesickness in Paris," *The Literary Digest* C/1 (Jan 5, 1929), **308**
22-23.

JESSEL, George. *This Way, Miss,* with a foreword by William Saroyan. **309**
NY: Henry Holt, 1955. 228 pp.
Contains a tribute to the composer.

JOHNSON, Harold Earle. *Symphony Hall, Boston* (Boston: Little, **310**
Brown, 1950), 126-27, 339, 405.
Information about Gershwin's *Second Rhapsody,* given its world
premiere by George Gershwin with the Boston Symphony Orchestra,
Jan 29, 1932. See also: Philip HALE, No. **263**.

JOHNSON, J. Rosamond. "Emancipator of American Idioms," in: Merle **311**
ARMITAGE, ed, *George Gershwin* (NY: Longmans, Green, 1938),
65-71.

JONES, LeRoi. "Movie Review," *Jazz Review* II/10 (Nov 1959), 50-51. **312**
Critical comments about Samuel Goldwyn's movie *Porgy and Bess,*
and of the opera itself.

JONES, Max. "Gershwin Could Not Have Had a Finer Monument," **313**
Melody Maker XXVIII/996 (Oct 18, 1952), 3.
On *Porgy and Bess.*

K

*KAHN, Otto H. "George Gershwin and American Youth," in: Merle   **314**
ARMITAGE, ed, *George Gershwin* (NY: Longmans, Green, 1938),
126-28. Excerpts originally appeared in the *Musical Courier*
XCVIII/1 (Jan 3, 1929), 31.

*KAUFMAN, George S., & Morrie RYSKIND. *Of Thee I Sing.* NY: A.A. **315**
Knopf, 1932. 214 pp.

*KAUFMAN, George S., & Morrie RYSKIND. *Let 'Em Eat Cake.* NY: **316**
A. A. Knopf, 1933. 241 pp.

KELLER, Hans. "Rhythm: Gershwin and Stravinsky," *Score and I.M.A.* **317**
Magazine No. 20 (June 1957), 19-31.
Examples of Gershwin's use of rhythm given.

KELLER, Hans. "Gershwin's Genius," *The Musical Times* CIII   **318**
[=No. 1437] (Nov 1962), 763-4.

KELLER, Hans. "Truth and Music," *Music and Musicians* XVI/2 (Oct **319**
1967), 16.

KENNEDY, John B. "Words and Music," *Colliers* LXXXII/12 (Sep 22, **320**
1928), 13.

KERN, Jerome. "Tribute," in: Merle ARMITAGE, ed, *George Gershwin* **321**
(NY: Longmans, Green, 1938), 120.

KERNOCHAN, Marshall. "Notable Music: Gershwin's 'Second Rhapsody' **322**
and 'Robin Hood'," *The Outlook and Independent* CLX/6 (Mar
1932), 196.

KERTESZ, Istvan. " 'Porgy es Bess'—Gershwin operájának bemutatója az **323**
Erkel Színházban," *Muzsika* XIII/3 (Apr 1970), 13-17.

KHACHATURIAN, Aram. "George Gershwin," *Uj zenei szemle* VI/12   **324**
(Dec 1955), 32-33.

KILENYI, Edward, Sr. "George Gershwin As I Knew Him," *Etude*   **325**
LXVIII/10 (Oct 1950), 11-12, 64.
Reminiscences by one of Gershwin's teachers.

KILENYI, Edward, Sr. *Gershwiniana: Recollections and Reminiscences* **326**
of Times Spent with My Student George Gershwin. Typescript:
n.p., 1962-63. 89 pp.
A partisan account of Gershwin's studies with the author.

KILLICK, John. "An Open Letter to Hans Keller," *American Musical* **327**
Digest I/5 (1970), 12-13. Reprinted from *The Listener* (Jan 8, 1970).
Claims that Keller's program (Dec 29, 1969) of Gershwin's songs
fell below standards.

KIMBALL, Robert, & Alfred SIMON. *The Gershwins,* with an intro- **327a**
duction by Richard Rodgers. NY: Atheneum, 1973. 292 pp.
A pictorial biography of the Gershwins.

KIRBY, Fred. "Do It Again' Is Excellent Gershwin—But Disappoints," **328**
Billboard LXXXIII/10 (Mar 6, 1971), 28.

KNIGHT, Arthur. "Catfish Row in Todd-AO," *The Saturday Review* **329**
XLII/27 (July 4, 1959), 24-25.
Review of the motion picture *Porgy and Bess.*

KNIGHT, Arthur. "Musicals à la Mode," *The Saturday Review* XL/15 **330**
(Apr 13, 1957), 26.

KNIGHT, Arthur, & Eliot ELISOFON. *The Hollywood Style.* NY: **331**
Macmillan, 1969. 216 pp.
Contains a photo of Gershwin's sitting room.

KOCH, Howard. See: "Rhapsody in Blue," No. **481**.

KOLODIN, Irving. "*Porgy and Bess*: American Opera in the Theatre," **332**
Theatre Arts Monthly XIX/11 (Nov 1935), 853-65.

KOLODIN, Irving. "Charleston Revisited," *Saturday Review of* **333**
Literature XXXIV/39 (Sep 29, 1951), 50-51.
Record review of *Porgy and Bess.*

KOLODIN, Irving. "Music to My Ears: 'Porgy'," *Saturday Review of* **334**
Literature XXXVI/13 (Mar 28, 1953), 27-28.
About *Porgy and Bess.*

KOLODIN, Irving. "Porgy and Bess: A Symphonic Picture," *The*   **335**
Philharmonic-Symphony Society of New York [Program]
CXI (Jan 16, 1954), [6-7].

KOLODIN, Irving. "An American in Paris," *The Philharmonic-Symphony* **336**
Society of New York [Program] CXI (Mar 13, 1954), [7].

KOLODIN, Irving. "Paradox in Blue," *The Saturday Review* XXXIX/8   **337**
(Feb 25, 1956), 37, 60-61.

KOLODIN, Irving. "Catfish Row and Wilshire," *The Saturday Review*   **338**
XLII/24 (June 13, 1959), 52.
About the film *Porgy and Bess.*

KOLODIN, Irving. "Mid-Month Recordings: From George to George   **339**
with Love," *The Saturday Review* XLII/42 (Oct 17, 1959), 78-79.
Record review of songs.

KOLODIN, Irving. "The Gershwins' Two Astaires," *The Saturday Review* **340**
LIV/44 (Oct 30, 1971), 70.

KOLODZIEJSKA, D. "'Lancelot' w Berlinskiej Staatsoper 'Porgy and   **341**
Bess' w Komische Oper," *Ruch Muzyczny* XIV/14 (1970), 10-11.

KONEN, Valentina Džozefovna. "'Porgy i Bess' Spektakl amerikankoj   **342**
ruppy 'Evrimen opera'," *Sovetskaya Muzyka* XX/3 (Mar 1956),
118-22.

KONEN, Valentina Džozefovna. "Džordž Gersvin i ego opera,"   **343**
Sovetskaya Muzyka XXIII/3 (Mar 1959), 166-73.
About *Porgy and Bess.*

KONSULOVA, V. "Plodiv: 'Gershuin—67'," *Bulgarska Muzika* XIX/3   **344**
(Mar 1968), 62-64.
Review of *Concerto in F & Rhapsody in Blue.*

KOSTELANETZ, André. "George Gershwin—An American Composer,"   **345**
Music Clubs Magazine XXXI/4 (May 1952), 4+.
Discusses Gershwin's works.

*KOUSSEVITSKY, Serge. "Man and Musician," in: Merle ARMITAGE,   **346**
ed, *George Gershwin* (NY: Longmans, Green, 1938), 113-14.

KOVALYER, U. "The Russian Critic," *The Saturday Review* XXXIX/2 **347**
(Jan 14, 1956), 38.
About *Porgy and Bess* in Leningrad.

KRAMER, A. Walter. "I Do Not Think Jazz 'Belongs'," *Singing* I/9 **348**
(Sep 1926), 13-14.
Alleges Gershwin did not orchestrate *Concerto in F*.

KRAMER, Jonathan D. "Program Notes," *San Francisco Symphony* **349**
Program Notes (Mar 1967), 22-23.
Notes for *An American in Paris, Concerto in F, Porgy and Bess,*
& *Rhapsody in Blue*.

KUTNER, Nanette. "Portrait in Our Time," in: Merle ARMITAGE, ed, **350**
George Gershwin (NY: Longmans, Green, 1938), 235.

KUZNETSOVA, Irina. "Pyat' i odna," *Sovetskaya Muzyka* XXXII/4 **351**
(Apr 1968), 46-51.
About *Porgy and Bess*.

KYDRÝNSKI, Lucjan. *Gershwin,* 2nd ed. Krakow: Polskie **352**
Wydawnictwo Muzyczne, 1967. 1st ed, 1962. 202 pp.
A popular biography in Polish. RILM[67] 281.

L

LA PRADE, Ernest. "Program Notes," *[The New York] Symphony* **353**
Society Bulletin XIX/6 (Dec 2, 1925), [1-2].
Comments on *Concerto in F*.

LANCASTER, Albert. "George Gershwin," *Keynote* (Autumn 1946), **354**
21-22.

LANGLEY, Allan Lincoln. "The Gershwin Myth," *The American* **355**
Spectator I/2 (Dec 1932), 1-2.

"Larry Adler to Unveil Gershwin String Quartet at Edinburgh Festival," **356**
Variety CCXXXI/2 (June 5, 1963), 43.
Announcement of the projected premiere of *Lullaby* (1919), a
movement for string quartet as adapted by Adler for harmonica and
string quartet.

LASKY, Jesse L. See: "Rhapsody in Blue," No. **481**.

LAWRENCE, Gertrude. *A Star Danced.* Garden City, NY: Doubleday,   **357**
    Doran, 1945. 238 pp.
    Some reminiscences about Gershwin.

LAWTON, Dorothy. "Reading About Gershwin," in: *Rhapsody in Blue;* **358**
    the Jubilant Story of George Gershwin and His Music [Hollywood:
    Warner Bros, 1945], 18.

LEVANT, Oscar. "Variations on a Gershwin Theme," *Town and*   **359**
    Country XCIV/4,206 (Nov 1939), 58-61, 83-84.
    Typically Levant; witty and anecdotal.

LEVANT, Oscar. "My Life; Or the Story of George Gershwin," in his: **360**
    A Smattering of Ignorance (NY: Doubleday, Doran, 1940), 147-210.
    Levant's chapter on Gershwin is humorous and full of insight.

LEVIEN, Sonya. See: "Rhapsody in Blue," No. **481**.

LEVIN, Sylvan. "So How's Your Embouchure? 'Porgy' Pickup Orchs   **361**
    O' Seas Quite a Problem to a Meticulous Maestro," *Variety* CCII/5
    (Apr 4, 1956), 2+.

LEVINE, Henry. "Gershwin, Handy and the Blues," *Clavier* IX/7   **362**
    (Oct 1970), 10-20.
    Discusses various aspects of *Rhapsody in Blue,* including rhythm and
    piano fingering.

LEVINE, Irving R. "U.S.S.R. May Cite 'Porgy' as Evidence There's No **363**
    Iron Curtain for Arts," *Variety* CCI/4 (Dec 28, 1955), 1+.

LEVINGER, Henry W. "The Roaring Twenties: 1920-29," *Musical*   **364**
    Courier CLI/3 (Feb 1, 1955), 42-43.
    Interview with Eva Gauthier.

LEWINE, Richard. "An American in Paris," *Film Music* XI/2 (Nov-Dec **365**
    1951), 14-16.

LEYDI, Roberto. "George Gershwin e it 'Porgy and Bess'," *Il Diapason* **366**
    V/1 (Jan 1955), 15-23.

Libraries. See: FISK UNIVERSITY, No. **178**; THE LIBRARY OF CONGRESS, Nos. **75, 276, 367** & **621-29**; MUSEUM OF THE CITY OF NEW YORK, No. **407**; NEW YORK PUBLIC LIBRARY, No. **412**; UNIVERSITY OF GEORGIA, No. **608**; & YALE UNIVERSITY, No. **651**.

THE LIBRARY OF CONGRESS. See: Frank C. CAMPBELL, No.**74**; Richard S. HILL, No. **276**; & Edward N. WATERS, Nos. **621-29**.

"L[ibrary] of C[ongress] Gets George Gershwin Manuscripts," *Billboard* **367** LXV/10 (Mar 7, 1953), 18.

LIEBERSON, Goddard. *The Columbia Book of Musical Masterworks,* **368** introduction by Edward Wallerstein. NY: Allen, Towne & Heath, 1947. 546 pp.
Program notes for *An American in Paris, Concerto in F, Porgy and Bess,* & *Rhapsody in Blue*; formerly appeared in Columbia Masterwork albums.

LIEBLING, Leonard. "The George I Knew," in: Merle ARMITAGE, ed, **369** *George Gershwin* (NY: Longmans, Green, 1938), 123-25.

LIPSKY, Leon. "George Gershwin, Jazz Glorified," *The American* **370** *Hebrew* CXVIII/2 (Nov 20, 1925), 59, 67.

LIST, Kurt. "George Gershwin's Music," *Commentary* I/2 (Dec 1945), **371** 27-34.
A critical assessment of the composer's work.

"The Live Art of Music," *The Outlook* CXLII/2 (Jan 13, 1926), 47-48. **372**

LLOYD, Noel. See: Geoffrey PALMER, No. **427**.

"London Symphony Orchestra," *Musical Opinion* LXXXI [=No. 962] **373** (Dec 1957), 153.

LONGMIRE, John. *John Ireland: Portrait of a Friend.* London: John **374** Baker, 1969. 176 pp.
Praise for "The Man I Love" (p. 51).

LONGOLIUS, Christian. *George Gershwin.* Berlin/Halensee: Max Hesse **375** Verlag, 1959. 68 pp.

LUCRAFT, Howard. "Behind Music USA," *Music USA* LXXVI/3   **376**
(Mar 1959), 9.
Concerning the motion picture *Porgy and Bess.*

LÜTTWITZ, Heinrich von. "Armeleutedramen—In Schwarz und Weiss,"   **377**
Musica X/1 (Jan 1956), 82-83.
Review of *Porgy and Bess* at Düsseldorf.

LÜTTWITZ, Heinrich von. "Ein Musical von Gershwin," *Musica*   **378**
XVII/6 (Nov-Dec 1963), 281-82.
Performance of *Girl Crazy* at Düsseldorf.

LÜTTWITZ, Heinrich von. "Gelsenkirchen: 'Porgy and Bess' Ohne   **379**
Negerlarven," *Neue Zeitschrift für Musik* CXXXII/8 (Aug 1971),
439-41.

LYONS, Leonard. "New York Is a Great Place to Be . . . ," *The*   **380**
Saturday Review XLI/42 (Oct 18, 1958), 26, 46-47. (Answered by
Ira Gershwin, ". . . But I Wouldn't Want to Live There." See:
Ira GERSHWIN, No. **217**.)

M

McBRIDE, Mary Margaret. See: Paul WHITEMAN, No. **637**.

MABIE, Janet. "Rhapsody on Gershwin," *The Christian Science*   **381**
Monitor XXVII/219 (Aug 14, 1935), 3, 14. (In Weekly Magazine
Section.)

MAIER, Guy. "Adventures of a Piano Teacher," *Etude* LXIX/11   **382**
(Nov 1951), 26.
Discusses publication of *Rhapsody in Blue* for solo piano from
pianist's standpoint.

MALIPIERO, Riccardo. "Porgy and Bess," *La Biennale di Venezia*   **383**
No. 22 (1954), 36-38.

MALMBERG, Helge. "George Gershwin," in: *Sohlmans Musiklexicon,* **384**
4 vols (Stockholm: Sohlmans Förlag, 1951-52), II, 542-43.

MAMOULIAN, Rouben. "I Remember," in: Merle ARMITAGE, ed,   **385**
   George Gershwin (NY: Longmans, Green, 1938), 47-57.
   Reminiscences about Gershwin by the director of the first production
   of *Porgy and Bess.*

"The Man I Love," *The New Republic* XCI/1,181 (July 21, 1937),   **386**
   293-94.

MAREK, George. "Rhapsody in Blue–Twenty-Five Years After,"   **387**
   Good Housekeeping CXXVIII/2 (Feb 1949), 4+.

MARROCCO, W. Thomas.   See: Arthur C. EDWARDS, No. **142**.

"Master of Jazz," *The Commonweal* XXVI/13 (July 23, 1937), 316.   **388**

MELLERS, Wilfrid. "Gershwin's Achievements," *The Monthly Musical*   **389**
   Record LXXXIII [=No. 943] (Jan 1953), 13-16.
   Comments on Gershwin's flair for writing "commercial" music.

MELLERS, Wilfrid. "Music, Theatre, and Commerce; a Note on   **390**
   Gershwin, Menotti and Marc Blitzstein," *The Score and I.M.A.*
   Magazine No. 12 (June 1955), 70-71.

MELLERS, Wilfrid. *Music in a New Found Land.* NY: A. A. Knopf,   **391**
   1965. 543 pp. 1st ed, London: Barrie & Rockliff, 1964.
   Gives much attention to Gershwin's music.

MERMAN, Ethel. *Who Could Ask For Anything More,* as told to Pete   **392**
   Martin. NY: Doubleday, 1955. 252 pp.
   Includes a story of her audition with Gershwin for a role in
   Girl Crazy of 1930.

"Miami U's Gershwin Fest to Revue One-Act Opera '135th Street' &   **393**
   Other Works," *Variety* CCLX/9 (Oct 14, 1970), 58.
   Announcement of Gershwin festival.

MILA, Massimo. "Lettera da Venezia: 'Porgy and Bess' di Gershwin,"   **394**
   La Rassegna Musicale XXIV/4 (Oct-Dec 1954), 349-51.

MILLER, Mayne. "Er Komponierte 'Porgy and Bess'," *Musikalische*   **395**
   Jugend XVI/3 (1967), 14.

MINGOTTI, Antonio. *Gershwin: Eine Bildbiographie.* Munich: Kindler,   **396**
1958. 143 pp.

A pictorial biography.

MITCHELL, Donald. "Concerts and Opera: [Some First Performances]," **397**
The Musical Times XCVII [=No. 1361] (July 1956), 374-75.

Review of *Lady Be Good.*

MONTAGU, George. "Musical Survey," *London Musical Events* VII/12   **398**
(Dec 1952), 37-38.

About *Porgy and Bess.*

MONTGOMERY, Michael. "George Gershwin Piano-Rollography,"   **399**
Record Research No. 42 (Mar-Apr 1962), 3-4.

A compilation of 114 record rolls Gershwin made for different labels
under various pseudonyms.

MONTSALVATGE, Xavier de. "Los conciertos en Barcelona," *Musica*   **400**
[Madrid] IV/1 (Jan-Mar 1955), 107-8.

Reviews *Porgy and Bess.*

MOOR, Paul. "'Porgy' Comes to Germany," *High Fidelity/Musical*   **401**
America XX/8 (Aug 1970), Sec II, 28-29.

MORGAN, Alfred Lindsay. "New Musical Heights in Radio," *Etude*   **402**
LX/12 (Dec 1942), 806.

About *Rhapsody in Blue.*

MORGAN, Alfred Lindsay. "A Famous Radio Debut," *Etude* LXII/4   **403**
(Apr 1944), 202, 252.

Cites Arturo Toscanini's performance of *Concerto in F* with the
NBC Symphony Orchestra, with Oscar Levant as soloist.

MORGENSTERN, Sam, ed. "George Gershwin, 1898-1937," in his: **404**
Composers on Music: An Anthology of Composers' Writings from
Palestrina to Copland (NY: Pantheon, 1956), 510-13. Also:
Schoenberg's remarks, 384-86.

"The Most Potent Musical Forces of the First Half of the Twentieth   **405**
Century," *Etude* LXIX/1 (Jan 1951), 9-11, 47-48.

Based on an opinion poll of prominent performers and composers,
Gershwin ranks among the top musicians selected.

"Muenchen," *Oper und Konzert* IX/4 (Apr 1971), 19-20.   **406**
   Review of *Porgy and Bess* in Munich.

MUSEUM OF THE CITY OF NEW YORK. *A Catalogue of the*   **407**
   Exhibition Gershwin: George the Music, Ira the Words. NY: Museum
   of the City of New York, 1968. 30 pp.
   Exhibition catalog, May 6-Sep 2, 1968; lists memorabilia, manuscripts,
   letters, drawings, scenic designs, etc. RILM 69 2923.

"–Music by Gershwin," *Music Clubs Magazine* XL/3 (Feb 1968), 14-15. **408**

"Music by Slide Rule," *News-Week* XXIV/13 (Sep 25, 1944), 80-82.   **409**
   Discusses Gershwin's studies with Schillinger.

N

NASHVILLE. See: FISK UNIVERSITY, No. **178**.

"The New Etude Gallery of Musical Celebrities," *Etude* XLVII/3 (Mar   **410**
   1929), 193-94.
   Portrait & brief biography.

"New Gershwin Tunes Featured in Movie," *Down Beat* XXXI/10   **411**
   (Apr 23, 1964), 14-15.
   About three posthumous Gershwin songs in Billy Wilder's
   Kiss Me Stupid.

NEW HAVEN. See: YALE UNIVERSITY, No. **651**.

NEW YORK. See: MUSEUM OF THE CITY OF NEW YORK, No. **407**;
   & NEW YORK PUBLIC LIBRARY, No. **412**.

NEW YORK PUBLIC LIBRARY. Library Museum for the Performing   **412**
   Arts, Lincoln Center.
   Materials on George and Ira Gershwin can be found in the Theater,
   Music (including Americana), Dance, Record, and Reference
   Collections; special materials include scores, programs, recordings,
   reviews, iconography, clipping files, etc.

NEWELL, George. "George Gershwin and Jazz," *The Outlook*   **413**
   CXLVIII/9 (Feb 29, 1928), 342-43, 351.

NICHOLS, Beverley. *Are They the Same at Home? Being a Series of*   **414**
    Bouquets Diffidently Distributed. NY: Doubleday, Doran, 1927.
    302 pp. Also as: "George Gershwin," in: Merle ARMITAGE, ed,
    George Gershwin (NY: Longmans, Green, 1938), 231-34.

    Among impressions of eminent people is an essay on Gershwin.

NILES, Abbe. "The Ewe Lamb of Widow Jazz," *The New Republic*   **415**
    XLIX/630 (Dec 29, 1926), 164-66.

NILES, Abbe. "A Note on Gershwin," *The Nation* CXXVIII/3319   **416**
    (Feb 13, 1929), 193-94.

"No Credit," *Musical America* LXXIX/8 (July 1959), 10.   **417**

    No singers given credit for dubbed voices in film version of *Porgy
    and Bess.*

*NOGUCHI, Isamu. "Portrait," in: Merle ARMITAGE, ed, *George*   **418**
    Gershwin (NY: Longmans, Green, 1938), 209-10.

O

O'CONNELL, Charles. *The Victor Book of Overtures, Tone Poems, and*   **419**
    Other Orchestral Works. NY: Simon & Schuster, 1950. 614 pp.

    Program notes for *An American in Paris.*

"Odyssey With Gershwin," *Newsweek* XLVII/2 (Jan 9, 1956), 43-44.   **420**

    Review of *Porgy and Bess.*

"Oh, Kay!" *Variety* CCXVIII/10 (May 4, 1960), 60.   **421**

    Review of an off-Broadway production of the musical.

O'HARA, John. "An American in Memoriam," *News-Week* XVI/3   **422**
    (July 15, 1940), 34.

    Tribute to Gershwin.

ONNEN, Frank. "Georges Gershwins Opera 'Porgy and Bess'," *Mens*   **423**
    en Melodie VIII/4 (Apr 1953), 117-19.

ORMSBEE, Helen. "New Broadway Star: Leontyne Price's 'Bess' Caps   **424**
    Her Lucky Year," *New York Herald Tribune* CXIII/38,885 (May 3,
    1953), Sec IV, 2.

OSGOOD, Henry Osborne. "The Jazz Bugaboo," *The American*   **425**
    Mercury VI [No. 23] (Nov 1925), 328-30.

Provides background for *Rhapsody in Blue.*

*OSGOOD, Henry Osborne. *So This Is Jazz.* Boston: Little, Brown, 1926. **426**
    258 pp.

Excellent source of information about the genesis and premiere of
Concerto in F & *Rhapsody in Blue*; see especially chapters 11-17,
which provide many details about *Rhapsody in Blue* and "Gershwin,
the White Hope."

P

PALMER, Geoffrey, & Noel LLOYD. *Music Tells the Tale, A Guide to*   **427**
    Programme Music. London/NY: Frederick Warne, 1967.

Program notes for *An American in Paris.*

"Paris 'Porgy' Hung Just in Time After Channel Storm Delay for Boff   **428**
    Debut," *Variety* CLXXXIX/11 (Feb 18, 1953), 57-58.

PARMENTER, Ross. "'Porgy' Singers Heard," *The New York Times*   **429**
    CII/34,876 (July 20, 1953), 14.

PARMENTER, Ross. "'Porgy' Group Ends Its Recital Series," *The New* **430**
    York Times CII/34,918 (Aug 31, 1953), 22.

PASI, Mario. *George Gershwin.* Parma: Guanda, 1958. 153 pp. Czech **431**
    translation as: *George Gershwin.* Prague: Statni hudebni vyd,
    1964. 126 pp.

PAUL, Elliot. See: "Rhapsody in Blue," No. **481**.

PAYNE, Pierre Stephen Robert. *Gershwin.* NY: Pyramid Books, 1960.   **432**
    157 pp.

Emphasizes the Jewish quality in Gershwin's music; not always
convincing.

PERKINS, Francis D. "'Porgy' Singers Give Last Concert," *New York*   **433**
    Herald Tribune CXIII/39,005 (Aug 31, 1953), 7.

PERKINS, Francis D. "Concerts & Recitals: Paul Whiteman,"   **434**
     New York Herald Tribune CXIV/39,537 (Feb 14, 1955), 9.

PERRYMAN, William R. *Walter Damrosch: An Educational Force in*   **435**
     American Music. Ph.D. Dissertation: Indiana University (in progress).

PESTALOZZA, Luigi. "Il Mondo musicale di Gershwin," *L'Approdo*   **436**
     Musicale I/4 (Oct-Dec 1958), 24-45.

PEYSER, Herbert F. "[Review of *An American in Paris*]," *The New*   **437**
     York Telegram LXI/140 (Dec 14, 1928). Excerpt in: Nicolas
     SLONIMSKY (No. **536**), 105 & (No. **538**), 485.

"Ein Phänomen der Musikgeschichte; Popularität zur Unsterblichkeit   **438**
     [George Gershwin]," *Musikhandel* VI (1955), 250.

PINCHARD, Max. "La vocation irrestible de George Gershwin," *Musica*   **439**
     [Chaix] No. 80 (Nov 1960), 25-29.

PINCHERLE, Marc. "Porgy and Bess de Gershwin," *Les Annales*   **440**
     LXII [=No. 60] (1955), 25-34.

P[IRONTI], A[lberto]. "[Review of Rene Chalupt's] George Gershwin,   **441**
     le Musicien de la 'Rhapsody in Bleu'," *La Rassegna Musicale*
     XXI/2 (Apr 1951), 178-79.

PLATEK, Jakov Michajlovič. See: Lev G. GRIGOŘEV, No. **255**.

"Plush Gershwin Festival Set for '53 Longhair Tour with Blessing of   **442**
     Family," *Variety* CLXXXV/7 (Jan 23, 1952), 1+.
     Announcement of an American tour by the Gershwin Concert
     Orchestra.

POLLAK, Robert. "Gershwin," *The Magazine of Art* XXX/9 (Sep   **443**
     1937), 531, 588.
     Claims that Gershwin is not an American Mozart.

POOL, Rosey E. *Een Nieuw lied voor America; het leven van George*   **444**
     Gershwin (1898-1937). Amsterdam: Tilburg-Nederlands Boekhus,
     1951. 155 pp.

POOL, Rosey E. "Een nieuw lied voor Amerika," *Mens en Melodie* **445**
VIII/1 (Jan 1953), 28.

POPOV, Innokenty. "Russian Report: 'Porgy and Bess'," *Musical* **446**
Courier CLIII/4 (Mar 1, 1956), 7+.

"Porgy and Bess," *Opera* III/12 (Dec 1952), 710-18. **447**

"Porgy and Bess," *Musica* [Madrid] II/1-2 (Jan-June 1953), 148-49. **448**

"Porgy and Bess," *Mens en Melodie* X/7 (July 1955), 223-24. **449**

"Porgy and Bess," *Music USA* LXXVI/7 (July 1959), 35. **450**
Record review.

"Porgy and Bess: A Symphonic Picture [arranged by Robert Russell **451**
Bennett]," *Pittsburgh Symphony Program* (Nov 1942).

"Porgy and Bess; Bethlehems nyinspelning," *Orkester Journal* XXV **452**
(July-Aug 1957), 42-43.

"Porgy and Bess Hailed in Moscow," *Musical America* LXXVI/2 **453**
(Jan 15, 1956), 29.

"'Porgy and Bess' in Moscow," *Etude* LXXIV/3 (Mar 1956), 14-15. **454**
Picture display of Robert Breen's all-Negro troupe in Moscow.

"'Porgy and Bess' on Tour," *Theatre Arts* XXVII/11 (Nov 1943), **455**
677-78.

"'Porgy & Bess' Praised in Spain," *The New York Times* CIV/35,444 **456**
(Feb 8, 1955), 19.

"Porgy and Bess Touring Europe," *Musical America* LXXVI/4 (Feb 15, **457**
1956), 208.

"Porgy and Bess Tours Behind Iron Curtain," *Musical Courier* CLI/2 **458**
(Jan 15, 1955), 33.

"'Porgy' Going Ahead with Russian Trip Plans Despite Lack of U.S. Coin **459**
Aid," *Variety* CC/8 (Oct 26, 1955), 55+.

"'Porgy' in Leningrad," *Time* LXVII/2 (Jan 9, 1956), 51.   **460**
> About the *Porgy and Bess* tour in Russia.

"Porgy Into Opera," *Time* XXVI/14 (Sep 30, 1935), 49-50.   **461**

"Porgy Orgy," *Time* LX/16 (Oct 20, 1952), 48.   **462**

"Porgy Orgy (contd.)," *Time* LXVIII/10 (Mar 7, 1955), 83.   **463**

"'Porgy' Production Is Staged in Naples," *The New York Times*   **464**
CIV/35,452 (Feb 16, 1955), 26.

"'Porgy': the Play that Set a Pattern," *Theatre Arts* XXXIX/10 (Oct   **465**
1955), 33-64.
> Complete text, with numerous illustrations.

"'Porgy' Tix on Black Market as Musical Wows Vienna," *Variety*   **466**
CLXXXVIII/2 (Sep 17, 1952), 2+.

"'Porgy' to TV for 112G; Two-Parter," *Variety* CCV/4 (Dec 26, 1956),   **467**
1+.

"'Porgy' Trip to the USSR Delays 'Blues'; Will Tour Aussie and Later   **468**
China," *Variety* CC/1 (Sep 7, 1955), 65.

"Posthumous Exhibit Shows that Gershwin Knew Harmony on Canvas   **469**
Also," *News-Week* X/25 (Dec 20, 1937), 28.
> Comments on one-man show of Gershwin's paintings at the Marie
> Harriman Gallery in New York.

PRAWY, Marcel. "Made in U.S.A.," *Opera News* XVII/7 (Dec 15, 1952),   **470**
12-13.
> *Porgy and Bess* triumphs in Vienna.

"Proben zu Gershwins 'Porgy and Bess' in der Berliner Komischen Oper,"   **471**
Opernwelt XI/3 (Mar 1970), 8.
> Six photographs.

PRYOR, Thomas M. "Hollywood Dossier: 'Porgy and Bess' Heads for   **472**
Films—Addenda," *The New York Times* CVI/36,268 (May 12,
1957), Sec II, 5.

PRYOR, Thomas M. "Hollywood 'Porgy' Strife: Switch of Directors of **473**
Folk Opera Makes 'the Livin' a Little Uneasy—Anamorphic Lenses
Unveiled," *The New York Times* CVII/36,716 (Aug 3, 1958), Sec II,
5.

PUGLIARO, Maria Vittoria. *Rapsodia in blue; l'arte e l'amore nella vita* **474**
di George Gershwin. Turin: S.A.S., 1952. 135 pp.

PYKE, L. Allen, II. *Jazz, 1920-1927: An Analytical Study.* 2 vols. **475**
206 pp. Ph.D. Dissertation: State University of Iowa, 1962.
UM: 62-4988. *Dissertation Abstracts* XXIII/8 (Feb 1963), 2937-A.

R

RAYMOND, Jack. "Berlin Acclaims Guests from Catfish Row," *The* **476**
New York Times CII/34,581 (Sep 28, 1952), Sec II, 1, 3.
Review of *Porgy and Bess.*

RAYMOND, Jack. "'Porgy' Delights Belgrade Crowd," *The New York* **477**
Times CIV/35,391 (Dec 17, 1954), 36.

REIS, Claire. "George Gershwin," in her: *Composers in America:* **478**
Biographical Sketches of Living Composers, with a Record of Their
Works, 1912-1937 (NY: Macmillan, 1938), 112.

"Revive 'Porgy & Bess' in Estonia; Producer Studied African Lore," **479**
Variety CCXLV/13 (Feb 15, 1967), 22.

REYNA, Ferdinando. "Adesso anche a Parigi," *La Scala* No. 42 (May **480**
1953), 38-42.

"Rhapsody in Blue," Screen Play by Howard Koch and Elliot Paul, **481**
Based on Original Screen Story by Sonya Levien. Producer: Jesse
L. Lasky. [Hollywood, Calif: Warner Bros. Pictures, 1945.]
151 pp.
Shooting script of movie; includes cast.

"Rhapsody in Blue," *The New York Times* XCIV/31,907 (June 3, 1945), **482**
Sec VI (Magazine), 24-25.
Shows scenes from the film *Porgy and Bess.*

"Rhapsody in Blue," *Musical Opinion* LXXX [=No.956] (June 1957),   **483**
537.

> Discusses miniature score of Grofé's arrangement of *Rhapsody* for
> symphony orchestra, published in England by Chappell.

"Rhapsody in Blue, for Piano and Orchestra," *Cincinnati Symphony*   **484**
Orchestra Program Notes (Feb 16, 1951), 509-11.

"Rhapsody in Blue, for Piano and Orchestra," *Philadelphia Orchestra*   **485**
Program Notes (Dec 7, 1951), 211.

"Rhapsody in Blue"; The Jubilant Story of George Gershwin and His   **486**
Music [Hollywood: Warner Bros, 1945] .

> A promotional pamphlet containing statements by Marion BAUER
> (See: No. **31**), Frank CROWNINSHIELD (See: No. **101**), Walter
> DAMROSCH (See: No. **108**), José ITURBI (See: No. **293**),
> Dorothy LAWTON (See: No. **358**), Artur RODZINSKI (See:
> No. **488**), Mark A. SCHUBART (See: No. **515**), Deems TAYLOR
> (See: No. **575**), and Paul WHITEMAN (See: No. **635**).

ROBINSON, Edward. "George Gershwin; a Punster Turned Poet,"   **487**
The Fortnightly Musical Revue II/1 (Oct 31, 1928), 3-4.

RODZINSKI, Artur. "George Gershwin," in: *Rhapsody in Blue; the*   **488**
Jubilant Story of George Gershwin and His Music [Hollywood:
Warner Bros, 1945] , 15.

ROLONTZ, Bob. "Gershwin Spec Misses Its Mark," *Billboard Music*   **489**
Week LXXIII/9 (Jan 23, 1961), 8.

ROSENFELD, Paul. "No Chabrier," *The New Republic* LXXIII/944   **490**
(Jan 4, 1933), 217-18.
Caustic assessment of Gershwin.

ROSENFELD, Paul. "Gershwin," in his: *Discoveries of a Music Critic*   **491**
(NY: Harcourt, Brace, 1936), 264-72, 384.
Critical evaluation of Gershwin's music.

ROSENFELD, John. "A New 'Porgy' in Dallas," *The Saturday Review*   **492**
of Literature XXXV/26 (June 28, 1952), 44.

ROSENWALD, Hans. "Speaking of Music," *Music News* XLII/4   **493**
(Apr 1950), 24.

RUBLOWSKY, John. "Gershwin and Ives: The Triumph of the Popular   **494**
Spirit," in his: *Music in America* (NY: Macmillan, 1967), 146-55.

RUBLOWSKY, John. *Popular Music* (NY: Basic Books, 1967), 56-57,   **495**
150.

RUSHMORE, Robert. *The Life of George Gershwin.* NY: Crowell-   **496**
Collier, 1966. 177 pp.

A biography for young people, grades 7-9.

RYSKIND, Morrie. See: George S. KAUFMAN, Nos. **315-16**.

S

SABIN, Robert. "Current Production of Porgy and Bess Justifies Its   **497**
Success Here and Abroad," *Musical America* LXXIII/6 (Apr 15,
1953), 33.

SABLOSKY, Irving. *American Music* (Chicago: University of Chicago   **498**
Press, 1969), 149-51, 154-55.

SAERCHINGER, César. "Jazz," *Musikblätter des Anbruch:*   **499**
Monatsschrift für moderne Musik VII/4 (Apr 1925), 205-10.

In this issue, devoted completely to jazz, the author writes about
Paul Whiteman's contributions, with special attention to *Rhapsody
in Blue.*

The Samuel Goldwyn Motion Picture Production of Porgy and Bess.   **500**
NY: Random House, 1959. Unpaged.

SANDOW, Hyman. "Gershwin to Write New Rhapsody," *Musical*   **501**
America XLVII/18 (Feb 18, 1928), 5.

Discusses Gershwin's plan to write *An American in Paris.*

SANDOW, Hyman. "Gershwin Presents a New Work," *Musical America*   **502**
XLVIII/18 (Aug 18, 1928), 5, 12.

Gives information about *An American in Paris* prior to its premiere.

SARGEANT, Winthrop. "Musical Events," *The New Yorker*   **503**
  XXXVIII/8 (Apr 14, 1962), 174-76.
  Review of *Porgy and Bess.*

. SAYLER, Oliver. See: George GERSHWIN, No. **210**.

SCHAEFER, Hansjürgen. *"Porgy und Bess* in der Komischen Oper   **504**
  Berlin," *Musik und Gesellschaft* XX/5 (May 1970), 325-28.
  RILM⁷⁰ 2282.

SCHAEFER, Theodore. "Gershwin Opera Heard in Capital," *Musical*   **505**
  America LXXII/14 (Nov 15, 1952), 23.

SCHERL, Adolph. "Gershwinova americká tragedie [Porgy and Bess],"   **506**
  Divadlo VII/4 (Apr 1956), 343-46.

SCHILLINGER, Frances. *Joseph Schillinger: A Memoir by His Wife.*   **507**
  NY: Greenberg, 1949. 224 pp.
  Touches on Gershwin's study with her husband.

SCHILLINGER, Joseph. *Kaleidophone.* NY: N. Witmark, 1940.   **508**
  Discusses Gershwin in his introduction to book.

SCHIPKE, Brigitte. *George Gershwin und die Welt seiner Musik.*   **509**
  Freiburg: Drei Ringe Musikverlag, 1955. 31 pp.

SCHNEERSON, Grigoriy M. "Preface," in: *Porgy and Bess* (Moscow: **510**
  State Publishers Music, 1965).
  Preface to a Russian edition of the score.

SCHOENBERG, Arnold. "George Gershwin," in: Merle ARMITAGE,   **511**
  ed, *George Gershwin* (NY: Longmans, Green, 1938), 97-98.
  Also in: Sam MORGENSTERN, ed, *Composers on Music: An*
  Anthology of Composers' Writings from Palestrina to Copland
  (NY: Pantheon, 1956), 384-86.
  Memorial tribute to Gershwin.

SCHOENBERG, Arnold. "A Self-Analysis," *Musical America* LXXIII/3   **512**
  (Feb 1953), 14, 172.
  Includes Gershwin's portrait of Schoenberg.

SCHOORL, Bob. *George Gershwin.* Amsterdam: A. J. G. Strengholt, **513**
    1952. 251 pp.

SCHROEDER, Juan German. "Porgy and Bess: Musica de George **514**
    Gershwin, Libreto du Bose Heyward," *Teatro; revista internacional
    de la escena* No. 15 (Mar-Apr 1955), 24-28.

SCHUBART, Mark A. "George Gershwin—Song Writer," in: *Rhapsody* **515**
    in Blue; the Jubilant Story of George Gershwin and His Music
    [Hollywood: Warner Bros, 1945] , 16.

SCHUMACH, Murray. "Hollywood Recall: Ira Gershwin Provides Notes **516**
    for 'Porgy'," *The New York Times* CVIII/37,038 (June 21, 1959),
    Sec II, 7.

SCHWARTZ, Charles M. *Elements of Jewish Music in Gershwin's* **517**
    Melody, M.A. Thesis: New York University, 1965. 71 pp.
    Examples given of Jewish style features in Gershwin's work.

SCHWARTZ, Charles M. *The Life and Orchestral Works of George* **518**
    Gershwin. 511 pp. Ph.D. Dissertation: New York University, 1969.
    UM: 70-3105. *Dissertation Abstracts* XXX/9 (Mar 1970), 3977-A.

SCHWARTZ, Charles M. "Gershwin," in: *Dictionary of Contemporary* **519**
    Music NY: E. P. Dutton, 1974.

*SCHWARTZ, Charles M. *GERSHWIN: His Life and Music,* with an **520**
    introduction by Leonard Bernstein. Indianapolis/NY: Bobbs-
    Merrill, 1973. 428 pp.

SCHWARZ, Boris. *Music and Musical Life in Soviet Russia, 1917-1970* **521**
    (NY: W. W. Norton; London: Barrie & Jenkins, 1972), 188, 293,
    357, 361, 443, 464.

SCHWINGER, Eckart. "Porgy and Bess," *Musica* XXIV/2 (Mar-Apr **522**
    1970), 148-49.
    Review of a Berlin performance of the opera.

SCHWINGER, Wolfram. "Notizen über Gershwin," *Musik und* **523**
    Gesellschaft X/5 (May 1960), 302-4.

SCHWINGER, Wolfram. *Er komponierte Amerika; George Gershwin,*   **524**
  Mensch und Werk. Berlin: Buchverlag Der Morgen, 1960. 222 pp.

SCULLY, Frank. "Scully's Scrapbook," *Variety* CCI/11 (Feb 15, 1956),   **525**
  73.
  Claims that *Porgy and Bess* is a greater popular success than *The
  Marriage of Figaro.*

SEAMAN, Julian. *Great Orchestral Music: A Treasury of Program Notes.*   **526**
  NY: Rinehart, 1950. (*The Field of Music Series,* Vol. 5)
  Program notes for *An American in Paris, Concerto in F, &
  Rhapsody in Blue*; cites numerous performances of Gershwin works.

SEDGWICK, Ruth Woodbury. See: Marcia DAVENPORT, No. **112**.

SELDEN-GOTH, Gisella. "Florence," *Musical Courier* CLII/7 (May   **527**
  1955), 31.
  Review of *Porgy and Bess.*

SELDES, Gilbert. *The Seven Lively Arts.* NY/London: Harper, 1924.   **528**
  398 pp.
  Discusses Gershwin favorably.

SELDES, Gilbert. "The Gershwin Case," in: Merle ARMITAGE, ed,   **529**
  George Gershwin (NY: Longmans, Green, 1938), 129-34.
  Reissued from *Esquire* II/5 (Oct 1934), 108, 130.
  Tribute to the composer.

SENDREY, Albert Heink. "Tennis Game," in: Merle ARMITAGE, ed,   **530**
  George Gershwin (NY: Longmans, Green, 1938), 102-12.

SHANLEY, J. P. "Newcomer Takes Bess Role Tonight," *The New York*   **531**
  Times CII/34,891 (Aug 4, 1953), 15.

SHAW, Arnold. "Gershwin, Arlen and the Blues," *Billboard* LXXIX/25   **532**
  (June 24, 1967), supplement, 68-69.

SHAWE-TAYLOR, Desmond. "Three Operas," *The New Statesman and*   **533**
  Nation XLIV/1128 (Oct 18, 1952), 448.
  Includes review of *Porgy and Bess.*

SHAWE-TAYLOR, Desmond. "A Mini-Success," *American Musical Digest* I/5 (1970), 12. Reprinted from the *London Sunday Times* (Jan 4, 1970).

SHNEERSON, Grigoriy. See: Grigoriy M. SCHNEERSON, No. **510**.

SIEGMEISTER, Elie, ed. *The Music Lover's Handbook* (NY: William Morrow, 1943), 728-29, 753-57, *et al.* See: George GERSHWIN, No. **212**; & John Tasker HOWARD, No. **283**.

SIMON, Alfred. See: Robert KIMBALL, No. **327a**.

SLONIMSKY, Nicolas. *Lexicon of Musical Invective* (NY: Coleman-Ross, 1953), 105. **536**

> Includes derogatory reviews of *An American in Paris, Porgy and Bess,* & *Rhapsody in Blue*, by Lawrence GILMAN (See: Nos. **229-30**), Herbert F. PEYSER (See: No. **437**), & Oscar THOMPSON (See: No. **582**).

SLONIMSKY, Nicolas. "Musical Oddities," *Etude* LXXIII/4 (Apr 1955), **537** 4-5.

> Includes an anecdote about Gershwin and Ravel.

SLONIMSKY, Nicolas. *Music Since 1900,* 4th ed (NY: Charles Scribner's, 1971), 111, 294, 384-85, 395, 404, 422-23, 439, 462, 484, 487, 512, 515, 535, 541, 543, 549-50, 552, 558, 573, 578, 610, 651, 660, 699, 801, 1002, 1433, 1476, 1497. 1st, 2nd & 3rd ed published by Coleman-Ross. **538**

> Documents numerous first performances of Gershwin works & quotes from several reviews; See: Olin DOWNES (No. **123**), Lawrence GILMAN (Nos. **229-30**), Herbert PEYSER (No. **437**), Deems TAYLOR (No. **572**), & Oscar THOMPSON (No. **582**).

SLONIMSKY, Nicolas. *Baker's Biographical Dictionary,* 5th ed (NY: G. Schirmer, 1968), 552-53. **539**

> Excellent dictionary article.

SMITH, Cecil M. *Musical Comedy in America.* NY: Theatre Arts Books, 1950. 374 pp. **540**

> Discusses Gershwin's major musical comedies.

SMITH, Julia. *Aaron Copland, His Work and Contribution to American*   **541**
    Music: A Study of the Development of His Musical Style and an
    Analysis of the Various Techniques of Writing He Has Employed in
    His Works. Ph.D. Dissertation: New York University, 1952. 664 pp.
    LC Mic: A53-246. UM: 4534. *Dissertation Abstracts* XIII/1 (July
    1953), 103-4-A. Published ed (NY: E. P. Dutton, 1955), 67-68,
    221, 248, 293.

SMITH, Marian Monta. *Six Miles to Dawn: An Analysis of the Modern*   **542**
    American Musical Comedy. Ph.D. Dissertation: Cornell University,
    1971. 212 pp. UM: 71-17,133. *Dissertation Abstracts* XXXII/1
    (July 1971), 587-A.
    Discusses *Of Thee I Sing* & *Porgy and Bess.*

SMOLIAN, Steven. *A Handbook of Film, Theatre, and Television Music*   **543**
    on Record, 1948-1969. NY: The Record Undertaker, 1970. 2 vols.
    64, 64 pp.
    Provides basic recording information for *An American in Paris,*
    Funny Face, Girl Crazy, Of Thee I Sing, Oh, Kay & *Porgy and Bess.*

SNEERSON, Grigoriy M. See: Grigoriy M. SCHNEERSON, No. **510**.

SORIA, Dorle J. "People and Places: Memorabilia to Go to Museum of   **544**
    the City of New York," *High Fidelity/Musical America* XVII/9
    (Sep 1967), MA-5.

SPAETH, Sigmund. "Our New Folk-Music," in his: *They Still Sing of*   **545**
    Love (NY: Horace Liveright, 1929), 173-78.
    Speaks of Gershwin's role of infusing serious music with jazz.

SPAETH, Sigmund. "Two Contemporary Americans: Gershwin and   **546**
    Hadley," *Scholastic* XXXII/12 (Apr 30, 1938), 23.

SPAETH, Sigmund. *A Guide to Great Orchestral Music.* NY: Modern   **547**
    Library, 1943. 532 pp.
    Program notes for *Concerto in F, Rhapsody in Blue* & *Second*
    Rhapsody.

SPAETH, Sigmund. *"Rhapsody in Blue" (The Story of George Gershwin).* **548**
    A Musical Study Outline of the Motion Picture by Warner Bros. for
    Music Clubs and Classes. [n.p.] :National Federation of Music Clubs,
    [1945].

SPAETH, Sigmund. *A History of Popular Music in America.* NY: **549**
Random House, 1948. 729 pp.

Discusses Gershwin songs and musical comedies.

SPAETH, Sigmund. "Theatre on the Disk," *Theatre Arts* XXXVIII/6   **550**
(June 1954), 10.

SPINGEL, Hans Otto. "Die Leute von der Catfish Row," *Opernwelt*   **551**
XI/4 (Apr 1970), 14-15.

Review of *Porgy and Bess* at Berlin Komische Oper, Jan 24, 1970.

SPITALNY, Evelyn. "First Gershwin Festival Rocks Miami U. Campus   **552**
with Music, not Mayhem," *Variety* CCLX/13 (Nov 11, 1970), 46.

STAMBLER, Irwin. *Encyclopedia of Popular Music* (NY: St. Martin's   **553**
Press, 1965), 87-90, 185, *et al.*

"A Steichen Gallery," *Opera News* XXXI/9 (Dec 24, 1966), 13.   **554**

Portrait of George Gershwin in 1927.

STEINERT, Alexander. "Porgy and Bess and Gershwin," in: Merle   **555**
ARMITAGE, ed, *George Gershwin* (NY: Longmans, Green, 1938),
43-46.

STEVENSON, Ronald. "Plenty o' Sump'n," *American Musical Digest*   **556**
I/5 (1970), 12. Excerpt from *The Listener* LXXXIII/2,128
(Jan 8, 1970), 58.

Review of Hans Keller's radio program (Dec 29, 1969), on
Gershwin's music.

STEWART, Lawrence D. See: Edward JABLONSKI, No. **304**.

STEWART, Ollie. "American Opera Conquers Europe," *Theatre Arts*   **557**
XXXIX/10 (Oct 1955), 30-32, 93-94.

"Stop the *Rhapsody*, Mab Told," *Down Beat* XVI/6 (Apr 8, 1949), 1.   **558**

Discusses legal action by Gershwin's publisher (Harms) to prevent
playing of an "unauthorized" arrangement of *Rhapsody in Blue*
by Charlie Barnet's band.

"The Story of George Gershwin, 1898-1937," *Music Journal* VIII/4   **559**
(Apr 1955), 17-18+. Summarized from the *New York Herald
Tribune* (July 12, 1937).

STRAVINSKY, Igor, & Robert CRAFT. "Some Composers: by Igor   **560**
Stravinsky with Robert Craft," *Musical America* LXXXII/6
(June 1962), 6, 8.
Stravinsky discusses his impressions of Gershwin.

STRAVINSKY, Igor, & Robert CRAFT. *Dialogues and a Diary*. Garden   **561**
City, NY: Doubleday, 1963. 279 pp.
Includes Stravinsky's comments in *Musical America* (June 1962).

"Student Production of 'Porgy and Bess'," *USSR* LVII/6 (June 1961),   **562**
60-61.
About the Russian production of *Porgy and Bess*.

SUTCLIFFE, James Helme. "East Berlin," *Opera News* XXXIV/20   **563**
(Mar 14, 1970), 32-34.
Review of *Porgy and Bess* at the Komische Oper.

SUTCLIFFE, James Helme. "West Berlin," *Opera* XXII/6 (June 1971),   **564**
535-37.
Review of *Porgy and Bess*.

SUTTON, Horace. "From Catfish Row to the Kremlin," *The Saturday*   **565**
Review XXXIX/2 (Jan 14, 1956), 37-38.
Review of *Porgy and Bess*.

SWIFT, Kay. "Gershwin and the Universal Touch," *Music of the West*   **566**
Magazine XV/2 (Oct 1959), 7, 24.
Comments favorably on Gershwin and *Porgy and Bess*.

T

T[RIMBLE], L[ester]. "Gershwin Night [at Hunter College]," *New   567
York Herald Tribune* CXIII/39,138 (Jan 11, 1954), 10.

TAMUSSINO, Ursula. "Gershwin Triumphiert über Mozart," *Phono:*   568
Internationale Schallplatten-Zeitschrift XII/2 (Mar-Apr 1965), 41+.
About *Porgy and Bess.*

TAUBMAN, Howard. "Why Gershwin's Tunes Live On: His Gift Was   569
That Out of Popular Themes He Could Arrive at Something
Memorable," *The New York Times* CII/34,581 (Sep 28, 1952),
Sec VI (Magazine Section-Sunday Edition), 20.

TAUBMAN, Howard. "After 20 Years: Gershwin Remains a Gifted   570
Composer Who Cultivated a Specific Garden," *The New York
Times* CVI/36,324 (July 7, 1957), Sec II, 7.
Tribute to Gershwin twenty years after his death.

TAYLOR, Deems. "Words and Music [review of *Rhapsody in Blue*]," 571
New York World LXIV/22,825 (Feb 17, 1924), 2-M (Metropolitan
Section). Excerpt in: Nicolas SLONIMSKY (No. **638**), 385.

TAYLOR, Deems. "[*An American in Paris*]," *The Philharmonic-*   572
Symphony Society of New York Program LXXXVI (Dec 13, 1928),
[5-8].
Gives the program for the tone poem.

TAYLOR, Deems. "Godfather to Polymnia," in his: *Of Men and Music* 573
(NY: Simon & Schuster, 1937), 144-53.
Primarily about Walter Damrosch; includes remarks about Damrosch's
influence on Gershwin.

TAYLOR, Deems. "Music and the Flag," in his: *Of Men and Music*   574
(NY: Simon & Schuster, 1937), 123-30.
Discusses the use of "national" style features, including jazz, in
serious music; cites Gershwin.

TAYLOR, Deems. "Gershwin as Pioneer," in: *Rhapsody in Blue; the*   575
Jubilant Story of George Gershwin and His Music [Hollywood:
Warner Bros, 1945], 13-14.

TAYLOR, Erma. "George Gershwin—A Lament," in: Merle   **576**
ARMITAGE, ed, *George Gershwin* (NY: Longmans, Green, 1938),
178-92. Reissued from *Jones' Magazine* (Nov 1937).

TEICHMANN, Howard. *George S. Kaufman: An Intimate Portrait.*   **577**
NY: Atheneum, 1972. 371 pp.

Contains a number of humorous anecdotes relating to Kaufman's
association with Gershwin.

TERPILOWSKI, Lech. " 'Trzeci nurt' a reminiscencje jazzowe w muzyce **578**
XX w," *Ruch Muzyczny* VI [=No. 13] (Jul 1962), 11-13.

TERRY, Walter. "World of Dance: 'G [eorge] B [allanchine] Boo-Boo'," **579**
The Saturday Review LIII/10 (Mar 7, 1970), 41.

Review of *Who Cares?*, Ballanchine-Gershwin ballet.

TEUTEBERG, Karin. "Gelsenkirchen," *Oper und Konzert* VIII/11   **580**
(Nov 1970), 9.

About *Porgy and Bess.*

THOMAS, Ernst. "America lebt in Strassen: Gershwins 'Porgy and Bess' **581**
in Frankfurt," *Neue Zeitschrift für Musik* CXVII/2 (Feb 1956),
90.

THOMAS, John Charles. See: Merle ARMITAGE, No. **10**.

THOMPSON, Oscar. "Gershwin's 'An American in Paris' Played for the **582**
First Time by the Philharmonic Symphony Orchestra," *New York
Evening Post* CXXVIII/24 (Dec 14, 1928), 15.

Review of world premiere of the tone poem. Excerpt in:
Nicolas SLONIMSKY, Nos. **536** & **538**.

THOMPSON, Oscar. *The International Cyclopedia of Music and*   **583**
Musicians, 9th ed (NY: Dodd, Mead, 1964), 785-86 (See: John
Tasker HOWARD, No. **282**).

THOMSON, Virgil. "George Gershwin," *Modern Music* XIII/1 (Nov-Dec **584**
1935), 13-19.

Critical comments on *Porgy and Bess.*

THOMSON, Virgil. *"Porgy* in Maplewood," in his: *The Musical Scene* **585**
(NY; A. A. Knopf, 1945), 167-69.

Reissue of a *New York Herald Tribune* review (Oct 19, 1941) of
the Maplewood, N.J., revival of *Porgy and Bess.*

THOMSON, Virgil. "It's About Time," in his: *The Musical Scene* **586**
(NY: A. A. Knopf, 1945), 17-19.

Reissue of a *New York Herald Tribune* review (Nov 2, 1942) of
the NBC Symphony Orchestra under Toscanini performing *Rhapsody
in Blue,* with Earl Wild & Benny Goodman as soloists.

THOMSON, Virgil. "Landscape with Music," in his: *The Musical Scene* **587**
(NY: A. A. Knopf, 1945), 25-28.

Reissue of a *New York Herald Tribune* review (July 11, 1943) of
a Hollywood Bowl performance of *Rhapsody in Blue* performed
by Paul Whiteman, with Ray Turner as pianist. Thomson is critical
of Ussher's program notes.

THOMSON, Virgil. *The Musical Scene* (NY: A. A. Knopf, 1945). **588**

Contains several Gershwin reviews; See: Nos. **585-87.**

THOMSON, Virgil. "Gershwin Black and Blue," in his: *The Art of* **589**
Judging Music (NY: A. A. Knopf, 1948), 55-56.

Reissue of a *New York Herald Tribune* review (Apr 19, 1946),
Rodzinski conducting the New York Philharmonic-Symphony
Orchestra in performance of *An American in Paris, Concerto in
F*, excerpts from *Porgy and Bess,* & *Rhapsody in Blue*, with
Oscar Levant as soloist.

THOMSON, Virgil. *The Art of Judging Music* (NY: A. A. Knopf, 1948), **590**
55-56.

Contains a review of an all-Gershwin program; See: No. **589.**

THOMSON, Virgil. "Expert and Original," in his: *Music Right and Left* **591**
(NY: Henry Holt, 1951), 14-16.

Reissue of a *New York Herald Tribune* review (Mar 9, 1950) of a
St. Louis Symphony Orchestra concert. Manuel Rosenthal's
Magic Manhattan is compared to Gershwin's *An American in Paris.*

THOMSON, Virgil. "English Landscape," in his: *Music Right and Left* **592**
    (NY: Henry Holt, 1951), 111-12.

> Reissue of a *New York Herald Tribune* review of Stokowski conducting
> the New York Philharmonic-Symphony Orchestra in a performance of
> the *Concerto in F*, with Byron Janis as pianist.

THOMSON, Virgil. *Music Right and Left* (NY: A. A. Knopf, 1951). **593**

> Contains several Gershwin reviews; See: Nos. **591-92**.

THOMSON, Virgil. *Virgil Thomson* (NY: A. A. Knopf, 1967), 151, 240, **594**
    242, 279, 405.

> Numerous passing remarks about Gershwin.

THOMSON, Virgil. *American Music Since 1910,* with an introduction by **595**
    Nicolas Nabokov (NY: Holt, Rinehart & Winston, 1971), 62, 63,
    146, *et al*.

> Numerous passing references.

TIPPETT, Michael. "The American Tradition," *American Musical Digest* **596**
    I/1 (Oct 1969), 21. Abridged from *The Listener* LXXXI/2,097
    (June 5, 1969), 804-5.

> Brief mention of Gershwin in an article about Charles Ives.

TODD, Arthur. "Theatre on the Disk: George Gershwin—American **597**
    Rhapsodist," *Theatre Arts* XXXVI/7 (July 1952), 10, 93.

> Includes a discography.

"Toscanini, All-American," *News-Week* XX/19 (Nov 9, 1942), 78. **598**

> About Arturo Toscanini performing *Rhapsody in Blue* on the radio.

"Transition," *News-Week* X/3 (July 17, 1937), 20. **599**

> Obituary.

TRAUBE, Leonard. "Charleston Gets Itself Plenty of Somethin' in Bow **600**
    of 'Porgy and Bess'," *Variety* CCLIX/7 (July 1, 1970), 1+.

"Trunkful of Tunes," *Newsweek* LXIII/9 (Mar 2, 1964), 48. **601**

> Discusses unpublished tunes Gershwin left behind.

TSCHULIK, Norbert. " 'Porgy and Bess' in der Volksoper," **602**
    Österreichische Musikzeitschrift XX/11 (Nov 1965), 599.

"TV Packagers Want Gershwin Musical Rights," *Billboard* LXIII/13   **603**
    (Mar 31, 1951), 17.

"Twenty Years After," *The New Yorker* XXXVIII/13 (May 17, 1952),   **604**
    26-27.
    About Ira Gershwin.

"The Twenty-Fifth Anniversary of the Premiere Performance,"   **605**
    Southwestern Musician XV/8 (Apr 1949), 31+.
    About *Rhapsody in Blue*.

TYNSON, Kh. "Geroi Gershvina na Estonskoy Stsene," *Sovetskaya*   **606**
    Muzyka XXXI/5 (May 1967), 45-48.
    About *Porgy and Bess*.

U

ULRICH, Homer. *Symphonic Music: Its Evolution Since the Renaissance*   **607**
    (NY: Columbia University Press, 1952), 321-22.
    Brief and general remarks on *An American in Paris, Concerto in F*
    & *Rhapsody in Blue*.

UNIVERSITY OF GEORGIA. Athens. Library, Department of Special   **608**
    Collections. Olin Downes Papers.
    These include an extensive file of Olin Downes' reviews as well as
    other reviews from *The New York Times* and the *New York*
    Herald Tribune. Included among the materials is a folder marked
    "George Gershwin," which contains a variety of printed items,
    including clippings, sundry pamphlets & programs.

"Unpublished Gershwin Songs to Be Released," *Variety* CCXXXIII/13   **609**
    (Feb 19, 1964), 51.
    Claims that approximately fifty unpublished Gershwin tunes in
    Ira Gershwin's possession will eventually be released.

UNTERMEYER, Louis. *Makers of the Modern World*. NY: Simon &   **610**
    Schuster, 1955. 809 pp.
    Considers Gershwin to be one of the four most important composers
    of the past century.

V

VALLEE, Rudy. "Troubadour's Tribute," in: Merle ARMITAGE, ed, **611**
George Gershwin (NY: Longmans, Green, 1938), 135-36.

VAN VECHTEN, Carl. "George Gershwin: An American Composer Who **612**
Is Writing Notable Music in the Jazz Idiom," *Vanity Fair* XXIV/1
(Mar 1925), 40, 78, 84.
Discusses Eva Gauthier's jazz concert and *Rhapsody in Blue*.

*VAN VECHTEN, Carl. "Introduction," in: Edward JABLONSKI & **613**
Lawrence D. STEWART, *The Gershwin Years* (Garden City, NY:
Doubleday, 1958), 21-26.

VAN VECHTEN, Carl. See: FISK UNIVERSITY, No. **178**.

VEINUS, Abraham. *The Concerto* (NY: Dover, 1964), 289-91. **614**
Reprint of a work first published by Doubleday, Doran, 1945.
Surveys Gershwin's influence on the concerto, with special
attention given to the *Concerto in F* & *Rhapsody in Blue*.

VEINUS, Abraham. *Victor Book of Concertos.* NY: Simon & Schuster, **615**
1948. 450 pp.
Program notes for *Concerto in F* & *Rhapsody in Blue*.

VERNON, Grenville. "Porgy and Bess," *The Commonweal* XXII/26 **616**
(Oct 25, 1935), 642.

VILLIUS, Lars. "Ålterblick på Gershwin," *Musikrevy* VIII/2 (Feb **617**
1953), 49-50.

W

WALDO, Fullerton. "High Spots in American Music," *Etude* LI/4 **618**
(Apr 1934), 23.
Passing mention of Gershwin; portrait.

WALKER, Raymond. "Down the Scale of Musical Memories," *Variety* **619**
CXCVI/7 (Oct 20, 1954), 50.
Touches on *Rhapsody in Blue*.

WALLGREN, Olle. "Goteborg," *Opera News* XXX/23 (Apr 9, 1966), 33. **620**
Review of *Porgy and Bess.*

WATERS, Edward N. "Gershwin's *Rhapsody in Blue,*" *The Library of* **621**
Congress Quarterly Journal of Acquisitions IV/3 (May 1947), 65-66.
A report of Ferde Grofé's gift of his own orchestration of Gershwin's
work; includes facsimile of two pages of music.

WATERS, Edward N. "Music," *The Library of Congress Quarterly* **622**
Journal of Current Acquisitions XVII/1 (Nov 1959), 19-50.
Discusses the gift of Gershwin's manuscript of *"I Got Rhythm"*
Variations, with facsimiles (pp. 23-24).

WATERS, Edward N. "Music," *The Library of Congress Quarterly* **623**
Journal of Current Acquisitions XVIII/1 (Nov 1960), 13-39.
Discusses gift of manuscript sketches for *Porgy and Bess* (p. 23).

WATERS, Edward N. "Harvest of the Year: Selected Acquisitions of **624**
the Music Division," *The Quarterly Journal of The Library of*
Congress XXIV/1 (Jan 1967), 47-82.
Reports gifts of Gershwin commemorative medals and a Russian
edition of *Porgy and Bess* (p. 79).

WATERS, Edward N. "Songs to Symphonies: Recent Acquisitions of **625**
the Music Division," *The Quarterly Journal of The Library of*
Congress XXV/1 (Jan 1968), 50-91.
Discusses gifts of three donors: Mrs. Kay Swift Galloway, and the
composer's two brothers, Ira and Arthur Gershwin. Gifts include
original manuscript of *The George Gershwin Song Book,* manuscript
fragments from the *Cuban Overture,* *"I Got Rhythm" Variations,*
Concerto in F, a music sketch book with Gershwin melodies, an
exercise book from Gershwin's studies with Edward Kilenyi, Sr.,
a brief student work, *Figured Choral,* an outline of the *"I Got*
Rhythm" Variations, and three exercise books from Gershwin's
study with Joseph Schillinger (pp. 53-55); also sundry letters and
other documents (p. 75).

WATERS, Edward N. "Paean to a Year of Plenty: Recent Acquisitions   **626**
   of the Music Division," *The Quarterly Journal of The Library of
   Congress* XXVI/1 (Jan 1969), 21-47.

   Reports gifts of a small sketchbook which Ira calls the "Red Tune
   Book" (p. 22); a collection of letters and personal papers with
   special emphasis on the musical play, *Lady in the Dark* [Ira Gershwin
   wrote lyrics; Kurt Weill composed music] (pp. 37 & 42).

WATERS, Edward N. "Variations on a Theme: Recent Acquisitions of   **627**
   the Music Division," *The Quarterly Journal of The Library of
   Congress* XXVII/1 (Jan 1970), 51-83.

   Describes Gershwin's exercise book from his study with Edward
   Kilenyi (p. 53), an Ira Gershwin autograph note (p. 68), and a
   560-page scrapbook from the period July 11-August 11, 1937,
   consisting of international articles and clippings related to Gershwin's
   terminal illness and death (p. 77). RILM[70] 53.

WATERS, Edward N. "Notable Music Acquisitions," *The Quarterly*   **628**
   Journal of The Library of Congress XXVIII/1 (Jan 1971), 45-72.

   Describes gift of *Lullaby* for string quartet; also sketches for
   Porgy and Bess (p. 46); also drafts of Ira Gershwin's piece for
   The Saturday Review, ". . . But I Wouldn't Want to Live There."
   (See: Ira GERSHWIN, No. **217**).

WATERS, Edward N. "Notable Acquisitions of the Music Division,"   **629**
   The Quarterly Journal of The Library of Congress XXIX/1
   (Jan 1972), 48-76.

   Describes gift of sketches for *Girl Crazy*, with Ira Gershwin's
   notes; sketches of *Porgy and Bess*; a notebook, *Themes*, with
   material used in *Rhapsody in Blue* and *Concerto in F* (p. 49);
   manuscript full score of *135th Street* with notes by Ira
   Gershwin (p. 61); Ira Gershwin gift of gold coins, including one
   of George Gershwin; score of a suite derived from *Porgy and
   Bess* called *Catfish Row*; also script from an interview on March
   13, 1933, over radio station WJZ (p. 64).

WATT, Douglas. "Popular Records: A Pair of Gershwins," *The New*   **630**
   Yorker XXXV/44 (Dec 19, 1959), 132-7.

WECHSBERG, Joseph. "Austria: 'Porgy' Makes a Hit," *Opera* XVI/12   **631**
   (Dec 1965), 899-901.

WECHSBERG, Joseph. "Vienna," *Opera News* XXX/6 (Dec 11, 1965),   **632**
32.
Review of *Porgy and Bess.*

WESTPHAL, Kurt. "Neue Musik in den Berliner Festwochen," *Melos*   **633**
XIX/11 (Nov 1952), 322-24.
About *Porgy and Bess.*

WHITEMAN, Paul. "George and the Rhapsody," in: Merle ARMITAGE, **634**
ed, *George Gershwin* (NY: Longmans, Green, 1938), 24-26.

WHITEMAN, Paul. "Rhapsody in Blue," in: *Rhapsody in Blue; the*   **635**
Jubilant Story of George Gershwin and His Music [Hollywood:
Warner Bros, 1945], 5-6.

WHITEMAN, Paul. "The Gershwin I Knew," *Music Journal* VIII/4   **636**
(Apr 1955), 19, 21.
Includes a discussion of *Rhapsody in Blue.*

WHITEMAN, Paul, & Mary Margaret McBRIDE. *Jazz.* NY: J. H. Sears,   **637**
1926. 298 pp.
Contains Whiteman's account of his role in the premiere of
Rhapsody in Blue.

WHITMAN, Alden. "Paul Whiteman, 'the Jazz King' of the Jazz Age,   **638**
Is Dead at 77," *The New York Times* CXVII/40,152 (Dec 30,
1967), 1, 24.
Summarizes Whiteman's career.

WIBORG, M. H. "Three Emperors of Broadway," *Art and Decorations*   **639**
XXIII/5 (May 1925), 48.

WIER, Albert, ed. *The Macmillan Encyclopedia of Music and Musicians*   **640**
(NY: Macmillan, 1938), 661.

WILDER, Alec. "George Gershwin (1898-1937)," in his: *American*   **641**
Popular Song (NY: Oxford University Press, 1972), 121-62.
An analytical study of Gershwin's songs.

WILSON, John S. "A Wide Variety of Porgys and Besses," *The New*   **642**
York Times CVIII/37,010 (May 24, 1959), Sec II, 15.
Record review.

WILSON, John S. "Ella Does Right by George," *The New York Times*   **643**
CIX/37,199 (Nov 29, 1959), Sec II, 19.
Record review of Ella Fitzgerald singing Gershwin.

WILSON, John S. "Ella Meets the Gershwins, with an Assist from   **644**
Nelson Riddle," *High Fidelity* X/1 (Jan 1960), 63-64.
Review of recording, "Ella Fitzgerald Sings the George and Ira
Gershwin Song Book."

WILSON, John S. "A Plaque in Brooklyn to Mark George Gershwin's   **645**
Birthplace," *The New York Times* CXIII/38,593 (Sep 23, 1963),
31.
Describes Gershwin's birthplace.

WILSON, John S. "Misunderstood Pioneer: Whiteman's 'King of Jazz'   **646**
Misnomer Obscured His Genuine Contribution," *The New York
Times* CXVII/40,152 (Dec 30, 1967), Sec II, 24.
An evaluation of Whiteman after his death.

WODEHOUSE, Pelham Grenville. See: Guy BOLTON, No. **46**.

WOOLLCOTT, Alexander. "George the Ingenuous," *Hearst's*   **647**
International-Cosmopolitan XCV/5 (Nov 1933), 32-33, 122-23.
Witty and anecdotal.

WORBS, Hans Christoph. *Welterfolge der modernen Oper.* Berlin: **648**
Rembrandt, 1967.
Discusses twenty-five major twentieth century operas, including
Porgy and Bess. RILM[68] 2271.

WÜRZ, Anton. "George Gershwin," in: Friedrich BLUME, ed, *Die*   **649**
Musik in Geschichte und Gegenwart, 14 vols (Kassel: Bärenreiter,
1949-), IV, col 1828-31.

WYATT, Euphemia. "American Opera," *The Catholic World* CLIV/924   **650**
(Mar 1942), 726-27.
About *Porgy and Bess.*

Y

YALE UNIVERSITY. Library. New Haven. James Waldon Johnson   **651**
Memorial Collection of Negro Arts & Letters.
Contains Gershwin-related material.

Z

ZEPP, Arthur. "I Was There—A View from the Servant's Quarters,"   **652**
Clavier X/2 (Feb 1971), 12-18.

ZIMEL, Heyman. "George Gershwin," *Young Israel* XX/10 (June 1928),   **653**
10-11.

ZOLOTOW, Sam. "Tibbett Goes on July 15th as 'Porgy'," *The New*   **654**
York Times CII/34,850 (June 24, 1953), 29.

DISCOGRAPHY

GEORGE GERSHWIN has not been neglected on records. His entree into the field of recorded music began in 1915 when, as a pianist, he started making player-piano rolls. Parenthetically, it should be noted that Gershwin recorded approximately 125 rolls (the exact number is still uncertain) between 1915 and 1926 under his own name as well as various pseudonyms—*i.e.*, Fred Murtha, Bert Wynn, and James Baker—for such labels as Universal Hand-Played, Metro-Art, Melodee, Perfection, Angelus, and Duo Art. It was not until Al Jolson recorded Gershwin's "Swanee" for Columbia Records in the early part of 1920 that the composer could claim his first record hit. As Gershwin's popularity increased during the past half century, it was inevitable that thousands of recordings of his music—some with the composer himself at the piano would be released. In such a climate of abundance, interpretation in performance and quality of sound reproduction vary widely. Furthermore, there has been a large turnover of recordings of Gershwin's works, for record companies, always sensitive to supply and demand factors, often drop discs of waning popularity from their catalogs in favor of new ones which presumably hold greater commercial promise. The field of recorded Gershwiniana is replete with records of one kind or another which have been taken out of circulation and are no longer readily available. Because of the need to select carefully from this inordinate quantity, a culled discography serves a wholly practical function, notwithstanding the inherent subjectivity of choice.

The Gershwin discography for this issue of *Bibliographies in American Music* is based on the record compilation prepared by this writer for his book *GERSHWIN: His Life and Music* (NY/Indianapolis: Bobbs-Merrill, 1973). Included are a few key 78 rpm recordings which are now collectors items. The balance of the compilation consists of LP recordings, not tapes or cassettes (neither of the latter are applicable for the recordings recommended). While some of the records cited (*e.g.*, Distinguished Recordings 107, or Archive of Piano Music X-914) were taken from piano rolls made by Gershwin, this discography does not list any piano-rolls (but see Michael Montgomery's "piano-rollography" in the main bibliographic section).

As a guide for the collector, the 78 rpm recordings are marked with an asterisk (*). Older LP recordings, of doubtful availability, are marked with two asterisks (**). More recent LP recordings—those which are presumably available or are listed in the current Schwann catalog—have no special indicator. All records cited are considered commendable, although those marked with a "+" are especially recommended.

For the purpose of identifying recordings, record numbers and letter designations (where applicable) have been given along with other pertinent information—especially details regarding performers and compositions. Record companies, however, frequently revise their number and letter designations as they change their catalogs to keep up with public demand. Inasmuch as it is almost as difficult to keep up with these revisions as it is to remain abreast of all of the latest audiophonic devices claimed by record manufacturers, the collector is advised to be prepared for occasional inconsistencies between a cited item and a "currently available" recording (this *caveat* is especially important in the light of discs newly released to celebrate the Gershwin anniversary). The basic descriptive information should suffice, however, to make the appropriate record choices.

For comparative purposes in making the best selection, the collector is urged to familiarize himself with other Gershwin discographies, such as those found in articles and biographies about the composer (*cf.* entries in the basic bibliography under Alan Dashiell, or Jablonski & Stewart). Discographic reference tools such as the Schwann catalog or, for earlier recordings through the mid-1950s, Clough and Cuming's *The World's Encyclopedia of Recorded Music* (London: Sidgwick & Jackson, 1952) as well as their *Second Supplement (1951-1952)* and *Third Supplement (1953-1955)*, can be very helpful. Also useful is *Record Ratings* compiled by Kurtz Myers and edited by Richard S. Hill (NY: Crown Publishers, 1956), an index of record reviews in periodicals through the mid-1950s. Reviews of current recordings, of course, may be found in such standard periodicals as *The American Record Guide*, *High Fidelity*, and *Stereo Review* (formerly *HiFi/Stereo Review*). Obviously these reference tools are only a starting point; the individual collector must ultimately decide which recordings best suit his personal taste.

Rhapsody in Blue (1924)

+Columbia MS-6091, MS-7518
> Columbia Symphony Orchestra, with Leonard Bernstein as pianist and conductor

Columbia MG-30073
> Philadelphia Orchestra, Eugene Ormandy, conductor, with Philippe Entremont as soloist

+*RCA Victor 55225-A
> Paul Whiteman's Orchestra, with George Gershwin as soloist (recorded June 10, 1924)

+*RCA Victor 35822
> Paul Whiteman's Orchestra, with George Gershwin as soloist (recorded April 21, 1927)

+**RCA Victor LPT-29
> Paul Whiteman's Orchestra, with George Gershwin as soloist (a 1951 reissue of the April 21, 1927 recording)

+RCA Victor LPV-555
> Paul Whiteman's Orchestra, with George Gershwin as soloist (a 1968 reissue of the April 21, 1927 recording)

**RCA Victor LM-6033
> Morton Gould's Orchestra, with Morton Gould as soloist

+Philips 6500118
> Monte Carlo Opera Orchestra, Edo de Waart, conductor, with Werner Hass as soloist

**Columbia CL-700, CS-8641
> Philadelphia Orchestra, Eugene Ormandy, conductor, with Oscar Levant as soloist

Turnabout TV-S 34457
> Berlin Symphony Orchestra, Samuel Adler, conductor, with Eugene List as soloist (in version based on the original one for piano and "jazz" ensemble)

**Mercury 90002
> Eastman-Rochester Orchestra, Howard Hanson, conductor, with Eugene List as soloist

RCA Victor LSC-2821
> Boston Pops Orchestra, Arthur Fiedler, conductor, with Peter Nero as pianist

Rhapsody in Blue   *continued*

Seraphim S-60174
>   Hollywood Bowl Symphony Orchestra, Felix Slatkin, conductor, with
>   Leonard Pennario as soloist

Columbia CS-8286
>   André Kostelanetz's Orchestra, with André Previn as soloist

Angel S-36810
>   London Symphony Orchestra, with André Previn as pianist and conductor

Everest 3067
>   Pittsburgh Symphony Orchestra, William Steinberg, conductor, with Jesús
>   Sanroma as soloist

RCA Victor LSC-2367, LSC-2746
>   Boston Pops Orchestra, Arthur Fiedler, conductor, with Earl Wild as soloist

+Archive of Piano Music X-914 (Everest Records)
>   George Gershwin as soloist (piano version)

+**Distinguished Recordings 107
>   George Gershwin as soloist (piano version)

+**RCA Victor LSP-2058, LPM-2058
>   George Gershwin as soloist (piano version)

Concerto in F (1925)

Columbia MG-30073
>   Philadelphia Orchestra, Eugene Ormandy, conductor, with Philippe
>   Entremont as soloist

**RCA Victor LM-6033
>   Morton Gould's Orchestra, with Morton Gould as soloist

Philips 6500118
>   Monte Carlo Opera Orchestra, Edo de Waart, conductor, with Werner Hass
>   as soloist

+**Columbia CL-700, CS-8641
>   New York Philharmonic, André Kostelanetz, conductor, with Oscar Levant
>   as soloist

**Mercury 90002
>   Eastman-Rochester Orchestra, Howard Hanson, conductor, with Eugene
>   List as soloist

RCA Victor LSC-3025
>   Boston Pops Orchestra, Arthur Fiedler, conductor, with Peter Nero as
>   pianist

Columbia CS-8286
  André Kostelanetz's Orchestra, with André Previn as soloist

Angel S-36810
  London Symphony Orchestra, with André Previn as pianist and conductor

RCA Victor LSC-2586
  Boston Pops Orchestra, Arthur Fiedler, conductor, with Earl Wild as pianist

Preludes for Piano (1926)

Nonesuch H-71284, HQ-1284
  William Bolcom

Concert Disc 217
  Frank Glazer

**RCA Victor LM-6033
  Morton Gould

RCA Victor LSC-2731, LSC-5001
  Leonard Pennario

Columbia MS-7518
  Oscar Levant

Turnabout TV-S 34457
  Eugene List

Golden Crest S-4065
  Grant Johannesen

An American in Paris (1928)

Vanguard C-10017, Westminster 8122
  Utah Symphony Orchestra, Maurice Abravanel, conductor

+Columbia MS-6091, MG-31155
  New York Philharmonic, Leonard Bernstein, conductor

**Mercury 90290
  Minneapolis Symphony Orchestra, Antal Dorati, conductor

RCA Victor LSC-2367, VICS-1423
  Boston Pops Orchestra, Arthur Fiedler, conductor

**RCA Victor LM-6033
  Morton Gould's Orchestra

An American in Paris *continued*

Columbia MG-30073, MS-7258, MS-7518
   Philadelphia Orchestra, Eugene Ormandy, conductor

Angel S-36810
   London Symphony Orchestra, André Previn, conductor

+*RCA Victor 35963/4
   RCA Victor Symphony Orchestra, Nathaniel Shilkret, conductor
   (recorded February 4, 1929)

+**RCA Victor LPT-29
   RCA Victor Symphony Orchestra, Nathaniel Shilkret, conductor
   (a 1951 reissue of the February 4, 1929 recording)

Seraphim S-60174
   Hollywood Bowl Symphony Orchestra, Felix Slatkin, conductor

Second Rhapsody (1931)

**Decca 8024
   Paul Whiteman's Orchestra, with Roy Bargy as soloist

**MGM E-3307
   Pro Musica Orchestra of Hamburg, Hans Jurgen Walther, conductor, with
   Sondra Bianca as soloist

**Columbia ML-2073
   Morton Gould's Orchestra, with Oscar Levant as soloist

Angel S-36070
   Hollywood Bowl Symphony Orchestra, Alfred Newman, conductor, with
   Leonard Pennario as soloist

Cuban Overture (1932)

RCA Victor LSC-2586
   Boston Pops Orchestra, Arthur Fiedler, conductor

**Mercury 90290
   Eastman-Rochester Orchestra, Howard Hanson, conductor

**Columbia ML-4481
   André Kostelanetz's Orchestra

**Epic BC-1047, LC-3626
   Cleveland Pops Orchestra, Louis Lane, conductor

"I Got Rhythm" Variations (1934)

**MGM E-3307
>   Pro Musica Orchestra of Hamburg, Hans Jurgen Walther, conductor, with Sondra Bianca as soloist

Philips 6500118
>   Monte Carlo Opera Orchestra, Edo de Waart, conductor, with Werner Hass as soloist

**Columbia ML-2073
>   Morton Gould's Orchestra, with Oscar Levant as soloist

Angel S-36070
>   Hollywood Bowl Symphony Orchestra, Alfred Newman, conductor, with Leonard Pennario as soloist

**Coral 57021
>   Paul Whiteman's Orchestra, with Buddy Weed as soloist

RCA Victor LSC-2586
>   Boston Pops Orchestra, Arthur Fiedler, conductor, with Earl Wild as soloist

Porgy and Bess (1935)

Complete Opera (with minor cuts)

+**Columbia OSL-162
>   Lawrence Winters, Camilla Williams, Inez Matthews, Avon Long, Warren Coleman, Edward Matthews, J. Rosamund Johnson Chorus, with Lehman Engel conducting the chorus and orchestra

Excerpts from the Opera (includes excerpts freely derived from score)

**Verve 64068
>   Louis Armstrong, Ella Fitzgerald, and orchestra

**RCA Victor LPM-3158
>   Cab Calloway, Helen Thigpen, and others

Columbia CS-8085
>   Miles Davis featured, orchestra conducted by Gil Evans

**Decca DL-78854
>   Sammy Davis, Jr., Carmen McRae, and orchestra

World Wide 20010
>   Douglas Singers, and orchestra

Porgy and Bess *continued*

+Decca DL-79024
> Todd Duncan, Anne Brown, the Eva Jessye Choir, and members of the original cast, with Alexander Smallens conducting the Decca Symphony Orchestra (a simulated stereo version of an earlier monaural recording)

+**RCA Victor LSC-2679
> Leontyne Price, William Warfield, McHenry Boatwright, and John W. Bubbles, with Skitch Henderson, conductor

**RCA Victor LM-1124
> Rïse Stevens, Robert Merrill, and the Robert Shaw Chorale

Orchestral Syntheses of the Opera

Catfish Row
(a five-movement suite from *Porgy and Bess*, by George Gershwin)

**Westminster 14063, 18850
> Utah Symphony Orchestra, Maurice Abravanel, conductor

A Symphonic Picture
(arranged by Robert Russell Bennett, conductor)

+RCA Victor VICS-1491
> RCA Symphony Orchestra, Robert Russell Bennett, conductor

**Mercury 90394
> Minneapolis Symphony Orchestra, Antal Dorati, conductor

RCA Victor LSC-3130
> Boston Pops Orchestra, Arthur Fiedler, conductor

Columbia MS-7258, MG-30073, MS-7518
> Philadelphia Orchestra, Eugene Ormandy, conductor

Command S-11307
> Pittsburgh Symphony Orchestra, William Steinberg, conductor

Porgy and Bess Suite
(arranged by Morton Gould)

**RCA Victor LM-6033
> Morton Gould's Orchestra

**"The Best of Astaire"   Epic LN-3137
Fred Astaire sings these Gershwin tunes from the movies *Shall We Dance* and *A Damsel in Distress*:

A Foggy Day
I Can't Be Bothered Now
Let's Call the Whole Thing Off
Nice Work If You Can Get It
Slap That Bass
They All Laughed
They Can't Take That Away from Me
Things Are Looking Up

**"Bing Crosby Sings Songs by George Gershwin"   Decca DL-5081

Embraceable You
I Got Plenty o' Nuttin
It Ain't Necessarily So
Love Walked In
Maybe
Somebody Loves Me
Summertime
They Can't Take That Away from Me

**"Columbia Album of George Gershwin"   (2 discs)   Columbia C2L-1
Percy Faith and his orchestra perform instrumental versions of these Gershwin works:

A Foggy Day
Bess, You Is My Woman
Bidin' My Time
Clap Yo' Hands
Embraceable You
Fascinating Rhythm
For You, For Me, For Evermore
I Got Plenty o' Nuttin
I Got Rhythm
Liza
Love Is Here to Stay
Maybe
Mine
My Man's Gone Now
Nice Work If You Can Get It
Preludes (Nos. 2 and 3)

"Columbia Album of George Gershwin"   *continued*

>   Somebody Loves Me
>   Someone to Watch over Me
>   Soon
>   Summertime
>   'S Wonderful
>   The Man I Love
>   They All Laughed
>   They Can't Take That Away from Me

**"Dorothy Kirsten Sings Songs of George Gershwin"   Columbia ML-2129
Dorothy Kirsten, with Percy Faith conducting the orchestra and chorus, sings:

>   Do, Do, Do
>   Embraceable You
>   I've Got a Crush on You
>   Love Is Here to Stay
>   Love Walked In
>   Mine
>   Someone to Watch over Me
>   Soon

+"Eddie Condon and Co., Vol. 1—Gershwin Program"   Decca DL-79234
A simulated stereo version of an earlier release ("George Gershwin Jazz Concert," Decca DL-5137) by Eddie Condon and his orchestra with Lee Wiley, Bobby Hackett, Jack Teagarden, Pee Wee Russell, Edmond Hall, Jess Stacy, and Joe Sullivan. They perform:

>   But Not for Me
>   Embraceable You
>   Fascinating Rhythm
>   I'll Build a Stairway to Paradise
>   My One and Only
>   Oh, Lady, Be Good!
>   Somebody Loves Me
>   Someone to Watch over Me
>   Summertime
>   Swanee
>   'S Wonderful
>   The Man I Love

**"Ella Fitzgerald Sings the George and Ira Gershwin Song Book" (5 discs)
Verve 629-5

Ella Fitzgerald, with Nelson Riddle conducting the orchestra, sings:

A Foggy Day
Aren't You Kind of Glad We Did?
Bidin' My Time
Boy Wanted
Boy! What Love Has Done to Me
But Not for Me
By Strauss
Embraceable You
Fascinating Rhythm
For You, For Me, For Evermore
Funny Face
He Loves and She Loves
How Long Has This Been Going On?
I Can't Be Bothered Now
I Got Rhythm
I Was Doing All Right
Isn't It a Pity?
I've Got a Crush on You
(I've Got) Beginner's Luck
Just Another Rhumba
Let's Call the Whole Thing Off
Let's Kiss and Make Up
Looking for a Boy
Lorelei
Love Is Here to Stay
Love Is Sweeping the Country
Love Walked In
My Cousin in Milwaukee
My One and Only
Nice Work If You Can Get It
Of Thee I Sing
Oh, Lady, Be Good!
Oh, So Nice
Sam and Delilah
Shall We Dance
Slap That Bass
Somebody from Somewhere
Someone to Watch over Me
Soon

"Ella Fitzgerald Sings the George and Ira Gershwin Song Book"   *continued*

Stiff Upper Lip
Strike Up the Band
'S Wonderful
That Certain Feeling
The Half of It, Dearie, Blues
The Man I Love
The Real American Folk Song
They All Laughed
They Can't Take That Away from Me
Things Are Looking Up
Treat Me Rough
You've Got What Gets Me
Who Cares?

**"Ella Sings Gershwin"   Decca 8378
Ella Fitzgerald sings:

But Not for Me
How Long Has This Been Going On?
I've Got a Crush on You
Looking for a Boy
Maybe
My One and Only
Nice Work If You Can Get It
Oh, Lady, Be Good!
Someone to Watch over Me
Soon

**"Embraceable You: A Tribute to George Gershwin"   Epic LG-1009
Wally Stotts and his orchestra perform:

Embraceable You
Liza
Love Is Here to Stay
Somebody Loves Me
Someone to Watch over Me
Strike Up the Band
Summertime
The Man I Love

+"George Gershwin Plays <u>Rhapsody in Blue</u> and Other Favorites" (recorded from piano rolls) Archive of Piano Music X-914 (Everest Records)
  Gershwin plays a piano version of the *Rhapsody in Blue*, and four selections by other composers:

> Grieving for You (Gold)
> Land Where the Good Songs Go (Kern)
> Make Believe (Shildkret)
> Some Sunday Morning (Whiting)

+"George Gershwin Revisited" Painted Smile PS-1357
  Barbara Cook, Bobby Short, Elaine Stritch, and Anthony Perkins, Norman Paris conducting the orchestra, perform thirteen Gershwin tunes, many of them relatively unknown:

> Changing My Tune (posthumous; *The Shocking Miss Pilgrim*, a 1946 film)
> Drifting Along with the Tide (*Scandals of 1921*)
> Feeling Sentimental (*Show Girl*, 1929)
> Oh Gee! Oh Joy! (*Rosalie*, 1928)
> Nashville Nightingale (*Nifties of 1923*)
> Rose of Madrid (*Scandals of 1924*)
> Scandal Walk (*Scandals of 1920*)
> The Back Bay Polka (posthumous; *The Shocking Miss Pilgrim*, 1946)
> There's More to the Kiss than the X-X-X (*Good Morning, Judge* and *La, La, Lucille* of 1919)
> Three Times a Day (*Tell Me More*, 1925)
> Tra-La-La (*For Goodness Sake*, 1922)
> Under a One-Man Top (*Sweet Little Devil*, 1924)
> Virginia Don't Go Too Far (*Sweet Little Devil*, 1924)

**"Gems from Gershwin" RCA Victor LPT-3055
  Jane Froman, Sunny Skylar, and Felix Knight, with Nathaniel Shilkret conducting the orchestra, perform 26 songs from *Girl Crazy*, *Lady, Be Good*, *Of Thee I Sing*, *Porgy and Bess*, and *Tip-Toes*.

> Bidin' My Time
> Clap Yo' Hands
> Do, Do, Do
> Do It Again
> Embraceable You
> Fascinating Rhythm
> I Got Plenty o' Nuttin
> I Got Rhythm
> Love Is Sweeping the Country

"Gems from Gershwin" *continued*

> Maybe
> My Man's Gone Now
> Of Thee I Sing
> Oh Gee! Oh Joy!
> Oh, Lady, Be Good!
> So Am I
> Somebody Loves Me
> Someone to Watch over Me
> South Sea Isle
> Strike Up the Band
> Summertime
> Swanee
> Sweet and Low-Down
> 'S Wonderful
> The Man I Love
> Wintergreen for President
> Who Cares?

+**"Gershwin Plays Gershwin"** Heritage H-0073

Gershwin as pianist and Fred Astaire perform:

> Clap Yo' Hands
> Do, Do, Do
> Fascinating Rhythm
> Hang on to Me
> I'd Rather Charleston
> Someone to Watch over Me
> Sweet and Low-Down
> That Certain Feeling
> The Half of It, Dearie, Blues

+**"Gershwin Plays Rhapsody in Blue"** (recorded from piano rolls) Distinguished Recordings 107

Gershwin as pianist plays the *Rhapsody in Blue* and three of his tunes: "Kickin' the Clouds Away," "Sweet and Low-Down," and "That Certain Feeling." He also performs Jerome Kern's "Left All Alone Again Blues" and "Whose Baby Are You?," Richard Whiting's "Ain't You Coming Back to Dixie?," and Sam Coslow's "Grieving for You."

**"Gershwin Rarities" (Volume 1)   Walden 302
Kaye Ballard, David Craig, and Betty Gillet, accompanied by pianists David
Baker and John Morris, perform:

Aren't You Kind of Glad We Did?
Funny Face
Isn't It a Pity
Kickin' the Clouds Away
Seventeen and Twenty-One
Shall We Dance
Soon
Stiff Upper Lip
They All Laughed
Things Are Looking Up

**"Gershwin Rarities" (Volume 2)   Walden 303
Louise Carlyle and Warren Galjour, accompanied by the John Morris Trio,
perform:

A Foggy Day
How Long Has This Been Going On?
I Want to Be a War Bride
Let's Kiss and Make Up
Oh, So Nice
Nice Work If You Can Get It
Nightie-Night
Sweet and Low-Down
That Certain Feeling
Where's the Boy? Here's the Girl!

**"The Gershwin Years" (3 discs)   Decca DXSZ-7160
Paula Stewart, Lynn Roberts, and Richard Hayes, with George Bassman
conducting the orchestra and chorus, perform:

A Foggy Day
Bess, You Is My Woman
Bidin' My Time
But Not for Me
Clap Yo' Hands
Could You Use Me?
Do, Do, Do
Do It Again
Do What You Do!
Embraceable You

"The Gershwin Years"   *continued*

Fascinating Rhythm
Feeling I'm Falling
He Loves and She Loves
High Hat
How Long Has This Been Going On?
I Don't Think I'll Fall in Love Today
I Got Rhythm
I Was So Young
I Won't Say I Will But I Won't Say I Won't
I'll Build a Stairway to Paradise
Isn't It a Pity?
I've Got a Crush on You
Let's Call the Whole Thing Off
Liza
Looking for a Boy
Lorelei
Love Is Here to Stay
Love Is Sweeping the Country
Love Walked In
Maybe
Mine
My Cousin in Milwaukee
My One and Only
Nice Work If You Can Get It
Nobody But You
Of Thee I Sing
Oh, Lady, Be Good!
Oh, So Nice
Rialto Ripples
So Am I
Some Wonderful Sort of Someone
Somebody Loves Me
Someone to Watch over Me
Soon
Summertime
Swanee
Sweet and Low-Down
'S Wonderful
That Certain Feeling
The Man I Love
There's a Boat Dat's Leavin' Soon for New York

They All Laughed
They Can't Take That Away from Me
When You Want 'Em, You Can't Get 'Em, When You Got 'Em, You
    Don't Want 'Em
Where's the Boy? Here's the Girl!
Who Cares?

"Heifetz Plays Gershwin and Music of France"   RCA Victor LSC-2586
Jascha Heifetz, with Brooks Smith at the piano, plays his transcriptions for
violin and piano of Gershwin's three *Preludes* as well as the following tunes
from *Porgy and Bess*:

A Woman Is a Sometime Thing
Bess, You Is My Woman
It Ain't Necessarily So
My Man's Gone Now
Summertime
Tempo di Blues (based on "There's a Boat Dat's Leavin' Soon for
    New York")

"Heifetz Encores" (Volume 2)   RCA Victor LSC-3256
Heifetz, with Brooks Smith at the piano, includes among his encores his
transcriptions for violin and piano of these tunes from *Porgy and Bess*:

Bess, You Is My Woman
It Ain't Necessarily So
Summertime

**"Music of George Gershwin"   Columbia AAL-39
George Gershwin, Fred Astaire, Larry Adler, and Hildegarde are heard in the
performance of:

Bess, You Is My Woman
Do, Do, Do
Fascinating Rhythm
I Got Plenty o' Nuttin
It Ain't Necessarily So
My One and Only
Summertime
Sweet and Low-Down
'S Wonderful
The Half of It, Dearie, Blues
The Man I Love
There's a Boat Dat's Leavin' Soon for New York

**"Music of George Gershwin"   Columbia ML-2026
André Kostelanetz and his orchestra perform instrumental versions of:

Embraceable You
Fascinating Rhythm
Maybe
Oh, Lady, Be Good!
Someone to Watch over Me
Soon
'S Wonderful
The Man I Love

**"Oscar Peterson and Buddy de Franco Play Gershwin"   Norgren MGM-1016
Pianist Oscar Peterson and clarinetist Buddy de Franco, with an orchestra
conducted by Russ Garcia, perform:

Bess, You Is My Woman
I Got Rhythm
It Ain't Necessarily So
I Was Doing All Right
Someone to Watch over Me
Strike Up the Band
'S Wonderful
The Man I Love
They Can't Take That Away from Me

+"Piano Music by George Gershwin"   Nonesuch H-71284, HQ-1284
William Bolcom performs a number of brief, essentially lightweight piano
pieces by Gershwin. They are "Rialto Ripples," an early piano rag (written in
conjunction with Will Donaldson and published in 1917), "Promenade,"
originally an instrumental interlude called "Walking the Dog" in the 1937
Astaire-Rogers movie *Shall We Dance*, "Jasbo Brown Blues" from *Porgy and
Bess* (retitled "Piano Playin' Jazzbo Brown"), and three little-known trifles
from the 1920s titled "Impromptu in Two Keys," "Merry Andrew," and
"Three-Quarter Blues." Bolcom also performs the three *Preludes for Piano*
and the composer's *Song-Book* of 1932, consisting of variations of eighteen
famous Gershwin tunes. The tunes of the *Song-Book*, in the order of
performance, are:

Swanee
Nobody But You
I'll Build a Stairway to Paradise
Do It Again
Fascinating Rhythm

Oh, Lady, Be Good!
Somebody Loves Me
Sweet and Low-Down
That Certain Feeling
The Man I Love
Clap Yo' Hands
Do, Do, Do
My One and Only
'S Wonderful
Strike Up the Band
Liza
I Got Rhythm
Who Cares?

+**"Piano Transcriptions of Eighteen Songs" Walden 200
Leonid Hambro performs Gershwin's *Song-Book*, with its variations of eighteen
Gershwin tunes (the tunes are listed under "Piano Music by George Gershwin").

**"The Popular Gershwin" (2 discs) RCA Victor LPM-6000
Frankie Carle, Eddie Fisher, Eartha Kitt, the Melachrino Strings, the Glenn
Miller Orchestra, Lou Monte, Jaye P. Morgan, the Henri René Orchestra, the
Sauter-Finegan Orchestra, Dinah Shore, the Hugo Winterhalter Orchestra, and
June Valli perform:

A Foggy Day
Bidin' My Time
But Not for Me
Do It Again
Embraceable You
Fascinating Rhythm
How Long Has This Been Going On?
I Got Rhythm
I'll Build a Stairway to Paradise
I've Got a Crush on You
Let's Call the Whole Thing Off
Liza
Looking for a Boy
Love Is Sweeping the Country
Love Walked In
Mine
Nice Work If You Can Get It

"The Popular Gershwin"   *continued*

Of Thee I Sing
Oh, Lady, Be Good!
Somebody Loves Me
Someone to Watch over Me
Song of the Flame
Strike Up the Band
Swanee
'S Wonderful
They All Laughed
They Can't Take That Away from Me
Who Cares?
Wintergreen for President

**"Sarah Vaughan Sings George Gershwin" (2 discs) Mercury MGP-2-101
Sarah Vaughan includes many of the verses for the Gershwin tunes in this
album. Hal Mooney conducts the orchestra. The songs:

A Foggy Day
Aren't You Kind of Glad We Did?
Bidin' My Time
Do It Again
He Loves and She Loves
How Long Has This Been Going On?
I Won't Say I Will But I Won't Say I Won't
I'll Build a Stairway to Paradise
Isn't It a Pity
I've Got a Crush on You
Let's Call the Whole Thing Off
Looking for a Boy
Lorelei
Love Walked In
My Man's Gone Now
My One and Only
Of Thee I Sing
Someone to Watch over Me
Summertime
The Man I Love
They All Laughed
Things Are Looking Up

" 'S Wonderful, 'S Marvelous, 'S Gershwin" Daybreak D R-2009
A recording made from a television special by that title which was presented
by Bell Telephone on NBC on January 17, 1972. Jack Lemmon, Fred Astaire,
Leslie Uggams, Peter Nero, Larry Kert, Robert Guillaume, Linda Bennett, and
the Elliot Lawrence Orchestra are heard in excerpts from *An American in
Paris*, *Concerto in F*, *Rhapsody in Blue*, and this potpourri of Gershwin tunes:

A Foggy Day
A Woman Is a Sometime Thing
Bess, You Is My Woman
But Not for Me
Embraceable You
Fascinating Rhythm
I Got Plenty o' Nuttin'
I Loves You, Porgy
I'll Build a Stairway to Paradise
It Ain't Necessarily So
I've Got a Crush on You
Let's Call the Whole Thing Off
Looking for a Boy
Love Is Here to Stay
My One and Only
Oh, Lady, Be Good!
Oh Lawd, I'm on My Way
Someone to Watch over Me
Strawberry Woman
'S Wonderful
The Man I Love
There's a Boat Dat's Leavin' Soon for New York
They All Laughed
They Can't Take That Away from Me

+Lady, Be Good (1924)   Monmouth-Evergreen MES-7036
Gershwin at the piano, Fred and Adele Astaire, and the Empire Orchestra perform seven tunes from the 1926 London production of this musical. These tunes were recorded during the London run. They are:

Fascinating Rhythm
Hang on to Me
I'd Rather Charleston
Oh, Lady, Be Good!
So Am I
Swiss Miss
The Half of It, Dearie, Blues

+Tip-Toes (1925)   Monmouth-Evergreen MES-7052
Allen Kearns, Dorothy Dickson, Laddie Cliff, Peggy Beatty, and Evan Thomas perform eight tunes from the 1926 London production of this musical. The tunes, recorded during the London run, are:

It's a Great Little World
Looking for a Boy
Nice Baby! (Come to Papa!)
Nightie-Night
Sweet and Low-Down
That Certain Feeling
These Charming People
When Do We Dance?

**Oh, Kay! (1926)   Columbia OL-7050, OS-2550, ACL-1050
Barbara Ruick, Jack Cassidy, Allen Case, Roger White, pianists Cy Walter and Bernard Leighton, and an orchestra and chorus conducted by Lehman Engel perform (in the order given):

Overture
The Woman's Touch
Don't Ask!
Dear Little Girl
Maybe
Clap Yo' Hands
Bride and Groom
Do, Do, Do
Someone to Watch over Me
Fidgety Feet
Heaven on Earth
Oh, Kay
Finale

+Funny Face (1927)   Monmouth-Evergreen MES-7037
This disc draws on the original cast recordings of the 1928 London
production of this musical as well as some piano solos by Gershwin that were
not part of the production. Gershwin at the piano, Fred and Adele Astaire,
Leslie Henson, and Bernard Clifton perform these tunes from the musical:

Funny Face
He Loves and She Loves
High Hat
My One and Only
'S Wonderful
Tell the Doc
The Babbitt and the Bromide

Girl Crazy (1930)   Columbia COS-2560
Mary Martin, Louise Carlyle, Eddie Chappell, and an orchestra and chorus
conducted by Lehman Engel perform (in the order given):

Overture and *Opening Chorus*
The Lonesome Cowboy
Bidin' My Time
Could You Use Me?
Broncho Busters
Barbary Coast
Embraceable You
Sam and Delilah
I Got Rhythm
But Not for Me
Treat Me Rough
Boy! What Love Has Done to Me!
When It's Cactus Time in Arizona
Finale

Of Thee I Sing (1931)   Columbia S-31763
A disc taken from the soundtrack of a television special presented on CBS on
October 24, 1972. Carroll O'Connor, Cloris Leachman, Jack Gilford, Michele
Lee, Jesse White, Jim Backus, Herb Edelman, Paul Hartman, and an orchestra
and chorus conducted by Peter Matz perform a shortened adaptation of the
score. Among the tunes heard between the *Overture* and *Finale* are:

Because, Because
I Was the Most Beautiful Blossom
I'm About to Be a Mother (Who Could Ask for Anything More?)
Jilted, Jilted!

Of Thee I Sing   *continued*

    Love Is Sweeping the Country
    Mine (from *Let 'Em Eat Cake*)
    Of Thee I Sing
    The Dimple on My Knee
    The Senatorial Roll Call
    Who Cares?
    Who Is the Lucky Girl to Be?
    Wintergreen for President

**Of Thee I Sing (1931)   Capitol S-350

    Jack Carson, Paul Hartman, Jack Whiting, Lenore Lonergan, and an orchestra
    and chorus conducted by Maurice Levine perform a 1952 version of the
    musical (based on a Broadway revival of that year).

**An American in Paris (1951)   MGM S-552 (a 1966 stereo-enhanced reissue of MGM E-93, a 1951 release)

Gene Kelly, Georges Guetary, and Johnny Green and the MGM Orchestra perform the film ballet sequence of *An American in Paris* as well as these tunes:

I Got Rhythm
I'll Build a Stairway to Paradise
Love Is Here to Stay
'S Wonderful

**Funny Face (1957)   Verve MGV-15001

Six tunes taken from the soundtrack of Paramount's movie version of the musical are performed by Fred Astaire, Audrey Hepburn, and Kay Thompson, with Adolph Deutsch conducting the orchestra. They sing:

Clap Yo' Hands
Funny Face
He Loves and She Loves
How Long Has This Been Going On?
Let's Kiss and Make Up
'S Wonderful

Porgy and Bess (1959)   Columbia OS 2016

Robert McFerrin and Adele Addison are the voices of Porgy and Bess—not Sidney Poitier and Dorothy Dandridge, as the record jacket would imply—in this recording taken from the soundtrack of Samuel Goldwyn's movie production of the opera (also Inez Matthew's voice was dubbed for Ruth Attaway, who played Serena in the movie, while Loulie Jean Norman sang for Diahann Carroll, who played Clara). André Previn conducts the orchestra and chorus. These selections are heard (in the order given):

Overture
Summertime
A Woman Is a Sometime Thing
Gone, Gone, Gone
My Man's Gone Now
I Got Plenty o' Nuttin'
Bess, You Is My Woman
Oh, I Can't Sit Down
It Ain't Necessarily So
I Ain' Got No Shame
What You Want wid Bess?
Strawberry Woman
Crab Man

Porgy and Bess   *continued*

I Loves You, Porgy
A Red Headed Woman
Clara, Clara (Don't You Be Downhearted)
There's a Boat Dat's Leavin' Soon for New York
Oh, Bess, Oh Where's My Bess?
Oh Lawd, I'm on My Way